JOE GILBERT

Advanced SEO

Copyright © 2023 by Joe Gilbert

All rights reserved. No part of this publication may be reproduced, stored or transmitted in any form or by any means, electronic, mechanical, photocopying, recording, scanning, or otherwise without written permission from the publisher. It is illegal to copy this book, post it to a website, or distribute it by any other means without permission.

First edition

*This book was professionally typeset on Reedsy.
Find out more at reedsy.com*

Contents

1	Foreword	1
2	About The Author	2
3	2024 update - what changed and where are we now?	5
4	The Fundamentals Of SEO	8
5	Is SEO Right For Everybody?	12
6	Creating An SEO Strategy	15
7	Understanding Google's Algorithms	18
8	Google's RankBrain	21
9	Local VS National SEO – What's The Difference?	23
10	The Art Of Reverse Engineering	26
11	Using SEOQuake To Analyze The Competition	30
12	Everything You Need To Know About Keyword Research	33
13	Understanding Search Intent to Get the Best Traffic	37
14	What Are LSA keywords?	40
15	Long-tail Keyword Phrases	43
16	Keyword Stuffing	46
17	SEO For E-Commerce Websites	49
18	Content is King	52
19	How Long Should a Page Be for SEO?	56
20	Avoiding Duplicate Content	59
21	The Skyscraper Method for SEO Content	62

22	Time to E-E-A-T	65
23	Understanding Google's YMYL Guidelines	69
24	All About Blogs	72
25	Topical Relevancy	76
26	What Role Do Images Play In SEO?	79
27	What Role Does Video Play In SEO?	82
28	The Growing Voice Search Trend	85
29	An Overview of On-page SEO	88
30	Correct Use of H1 and H2 Tags	91
31	How to Use RankMath for Wordpress SEO	94
32	Landing Pages – The Secret Weapon For Keyword Variation	99
33	Technical SEO	103
34	URL Structure for SEO	106
35	Domain Authority	109
36	Getting To Grips With Microschema	111
37	Understanding Website Engagement	113
38	Mastering Bounce Rate for Better SEO	116
39	Why Speed Matters	119
40	How to Speed Up Your WordPress Website	122
41	Internal Linking	125
42	Page Structure And Link Depth	128
43	All About Backlinks	131
44	How To Build High-Quality Backlinks	133
45	Cleaning Your Backlink Profile	137
46	Building Backlinks with Wikipedia to Boost SEO	141
47	How To Use HARO for Link Building	144
48	The Importance Of Deep Backlinks	146
49	Understanding Tiered Backlinks	149
50	Does linking out to other sites help SEO?	151

51	Building Citations	154
52	Follow Vs No-follow Backlinks	157
53	Google My Business	159
54	What Role Does Social Media Play In SEO?	162
55	Why Reviews Are So Important	165
56	Tracking Your Progress	168
57	Black-Hat SEO	171
58	My Favourite Tools	174
59	Using ChatGPT for SEO	178
60	The Future Of SEO	181

1

Foreword

SEO is the art of creating a digital masterpiece that stands the test of time. It's not just about climbing to the top of search engine rankings, but about crafting a brand that resonates with your audience and drives meaningful engagement.

It's a journey of continuous learning, experimentation, and adaptation, but the rewards are priceless - a sustainable online presence that grows and flourishes over time.

So embrace the challenge, keep an open mind, and let your creativity flow - for SEO is a canvas on which your digital legacy is painted.

~ Joe Gilbert

2

About The Author

My first introduction to Search Engine Optimisation (SEO) was when I graduated from university in 2010. It was the height of the recession, or "credit crunch" – and absolutely nobody was hiring architect grads at that time. So I decided to pursue my passion for photography and set about becoming a full-time professional wedding photographer. I'd already started this during my studying so I had an existing portfolio of work, but until now all my clients had found their way to me organically via word of mouth and referrals.

I left university with no money, no savings, and no income, other than the handful of weddings that I already had booked in for the coming months. I desperately needed bookings, but had no money to invest in paid advertising. Back then, Instagram and TikTok weren't around, and I didn't have time to build up a following on Facebook to slowly attract clients. I needed to get found, fast!

I concluded that if I could get my photography website found at the top of Google, I would be able to get my portfolio out in front of couples who were getting married and actively looking for a wedding photographer in the areas I covered, and best of all it wouldn't cost me any money – just time (and I had plenty of that!)

So I set to work learning all about search engine optimisation. I obsessively read articles and blogs, watched videos, subscribed to every SEO newsletter I could find, and consumed any other bit of content on SEO that was available to me. I would spend hours scrutinising the websites in the no.1 position, analysing how many words were on their pages, what length Meta Titles they used, how many images they had, how often they blogged, and how quickly the site loaded.

I figured that the websites who were sat at no.1 on Google offered me a ready-made blueprint on how to get to the top, and all I had to do was reverse engineer these sites and apply what I had learned to my site.

Slowly but surely my efforts proved successful, and within six months my website had ranked no.1 for "wedding photography kent." I would spend hours running experiments, tweaking things to see what results they would have on my website and measuring my findings.

I was telling my parents one day about my growing successes as a wedding photographer, and about how I'd learned all about Google's algorithms and how to get my website ranking at the top. They were intrigued, and asked if I could do the same thing for their counselling / therapy centre. I agreed, applied what I had learned to their website, and sure enough within 6 months of hard work my activities had paid off, and their website proudly sat in the no.1 position within their local area.

It then occurred to me that whilst I had learned SEO for my own benefits, I could do what I had learned for other people, and help other businesses also get found on Google. In 2015 I quit photography completely, and founded Red Giraffe Marketing LTD – a Digital Marketing agency specialising in SEO and Web Design. Since then we've helped hundreds of businesses get their website onto the first page of Google, with a 100% success rate. Red Giraffe is now one of the top-rated digital marketing agencies in the UK, and I have an outstanding, highly trained team working alongside me to deliver exceptional SEO results for our clients.

A lot has changed since I first leaned SEO all those years ago, but by staying on top of the algorithm updates and continuously learning and keeping up with the changes, we are able to deliver results with the same efficiency today as I did when I first learned SEO.

3

2024 update - what changed and where are we now?

SEO is constantly evolving, and 2024 is sure to be no different. Here are some of the biggest changes that we saw in the SEO industry in 2023, and what's likely to happen in 2024:

- **Focus on user intent and helpful content.** Google's 2023 Broad Core Algorithm Update was focused on prioritizing content that is helpful, reliable, and created with people in mind. This means that SEO practitioners need to focus on creating content that meets the specific needs of their target audience, rather than simply trying to rank for keywords.

- **Increased emphasis on E-E-A-T.** E-E-A-T, which stands for Experience, Expertise, Authoritativeness, and Trustworthiness, is a ranking factor that Google has been using for several years. However, in 2023, Google began to emphasize E-A-T even more. This means that SEO practitioners need to make sure that their content is created by experts in the field, and that their website is a trusted source of information.

- **Continued growth of mobile search.** Mobile search has been growing for years, and this trend continued in 2023. More and more people are using their smartphones and tablets to search the web, so SEO practitioners need to make sure that their websites are not only fast and mobile-friendly, but built from a mobile-first perspective.

- **Emergence of new technologies.** New technologies are constantly emerging that can impact SEO. For example, in 2023, we saw the rise of AI-generated content and voice search. SEO practitioners need to be aware of these new technologies and how they can be used to improve their SEO results.

- **More AI-powered SEO tools and services.** AI is already being used in a variety of ways in the SEO industry, and this trend is only going to accelerate in 2024. We can expect to see more AI-powered SEO tools and services emerge next year, which can help SEO practitioners to automate tasks, gain insights, and improve their SEO results.

Here are some specific tips for SEO practitioners in 2024:

- **Create content that is helpful, reliable, and created with people in mind.** Focus on understanding the search intent of your target audience and creating content that meets their specific needs.

- **Make sure that your content is created by experts in the field and that your website is a trusted source of information.** This will help you to improve your E-A-T score.

- **Stay up-to-date on the latest SEO trends and technologies.** New technologies are constantly emerging that can impact SEO, so it's important to be aware of them and how they can be used to improve your SEO results.

- **Explore AI-powered SEO tools and services.** AI can help you to automate tasks, gain insights, and improve your SEO results.

In addition to these general trends, we can also expect to see some specific changes to SEO in 2024. For example, we can expect to see Google continue to improve its ability to understand and rank voice search queries. We can also expect to see Google place greater emphasis on user experience factors, such as page speed and Core Web Vitals.

Overall, SEO in 2024 is likely to be even more competitive than it is today. However, by focusing on the trends and changes mentioned above, SEO practitioners can stay ahead of the curve and improve their chances of success.

By following these tips, you can set yourself up for success in the SEO landscape in 2024 and beyond.

4

The Fundamentals Of SEO

Before I teach you how to get to the top of Google, let's get one thing clear – this IS NOT about how to get to the top of Google! Let me explain...

In order to become great at SEO, we must first understand how Google works. SEO is not about manipulating Google; Google is not a mountain we can climb, there is no set path to the top, or a series of specific actions we can take. There are no hacks, secrets, shortcuts or magic solutions.

SEO is fundamentally about working on our relationship with Google; if we work hard enough and do enough for Google to like and trust us, Google rewards us by showing our website more favourably in the rankings. If we are able to build more trust, more credibility and demonstrate more expertise to Google than our competitors, Google shows our website above theirs. It's as simple as that. A lot has changed in the world of SEO since I first learned it all those years ago, but this much has never changed, and never will.

It's important you understand that Google cares deeply about its users and wants to offer them the best search engine experience on the market, which is why Google is the market leader. In order to offer the best experience, Google must deliver the best results, meaning showing its users websites that are credible, trustworthy, well-built, easy to navigate, quick to load, secure, and demonstrate clear knowledge and expertise.

If we lie to Google, cheat, try and game the system, or bend Google's algorithms to our will, Google will fall out with us, and penalize us in the form of reduced rankings. All work we do must always be genuine and authentic; Google is too smart to be fooled by those attempting quick wins and shortcuts.

So let's begin...

Search Engine Optimization (SEO) is a critical component of digital marketing that helps businesses improve their online presence and drive more traffic to their website. Whether you are just starting out with SEO or looking to improve your existing efforts, understanding the fundamental principles is essential. In this chapter, we'll cover the basics of SEO and the key principles you need to know to get started.

Understand Your Audience

The first step in any successful SEO strategy is to understand your target audience. You need to know who your ideal customer is, what their needs are, and what keywords they are likely to use when searching for your products or services. Once you have a clear understanding of your audience, you can tailor your content and SEO efforts to meet your needs.

Conduct Keyword Research

We'll go into more depth on this later, but essentially keyword research is the process of identifying the search terms and phrases that your audience is using to find products or services like yours. By conducting keyword research, you can optimize your website content and structure to target these keywords and improve your search engine rankings.

On-Page Optimization

On-page optimization refers to the optimization of individual web pages to improve your search engine rankings. This includes optimizing title tags, meta descriptions, header tags, and content for specific keywords. It's also important to ensure that your website is mobile-friendly and optimized for fast loading speeds.

Off-Page Optimization

Off-page optimization refers to activities that take place outside of your website to improve your search engine rankings. This includes building backlinks from high-quality, authoritative websites, and social media marketing. By building a strong off-page optimization strategy, you can improve your website's authority and credibility with search engines.

Analytics and Tracking

Finally, it's important to track and measure your SEO efforts to determine what is working and what needs improvement. By using analytics tools, you can monitor your website's traffic, track keyword rankings, and measure the success of your SEO campaigns. This data can help you make informed decisions about how to optimize your website and improve your search engine rankings.

Summary

SEO is a complex and ever-evolving discipline that requires a solid understanding of the fundamental principles. By focusing on understanding your audience, conducting keyword research, optimizing your website, building a strong backlink profile, and tracking your progress, you can improve your search engine rankings and drive more traffic to your website.

5

Is SEO Right For Everybody?

SEO is a valuable marketing strategy that can help you improve your online visibility and drive more traffic to your website. However, SEO may not be the right strategy for every business. Before taking on a new SEO client at Red Giraffe, we always conduct a feasibility study to see if SEO is right for their needs, and how likely they are to generate a return on investment.

Here are some factors to consider when deciding if SEO is right for your business.

Your Industry

Some industries are highly competitive and require a significant investment in SEO to see results. Other industries may not have as much competition, making it easier to see results with a smaller investment. Additionally, some industries may not benefit as much from SEO as others, depending on the purchasing behaviour of their target audience.

Your Business Goals

If your business goals include increasing your online visibility, driving more traffic to your website, and generating leads, then SEO can be a valuable strategy to help you achieve those goals.

However, if your business goals are focused on immediate sales and revenue, then other marketing strategies, such as pay-per-click advertising, may be a better fit.

Your Budget

SEO requires a significant investment in time, resources, and money. If your business has a limited budget, then you may need to prioritize other marketing strategies that can generate quicker results.

Your Website

In order for SEO to be effective, your website needs to be optimized for search engines. This includes having high-quality content, a user-friendly design, and a strong backlink profile. If your website is not currently optimized, then it may require additional investment in order to see results from SEO.

Your Timeline

SEO is a long-term strategy that requires patience and persistence. It can take several months to see results from SEO, and ongoing optimization is required to maintain and improve your website's rankings. If your business requires immediate results, then SEO may not be the best fit for your timeline.

Summary

While SEO can be a valuable marketing strategy for many businesses, it may not be the right fit for every business. Factors such as your industry, business goals, budget, website, and timeline should all be considered when deciding if SEO is right for your business. It's important to work with an experienced SEO professional who can help you assess your business needs and develop a customized SEO strategy that aligns with your goals and budget.

6

Creating An SEO Strategy

There's a lot covered in this book, and I appreciate it can seem overwhelming when you first take on a new website. I have personally always found breaking it down into chunks and producing a 90-day plan is a really great way of designing a manageable SEO strategy. A 90-day plan is a simple but effective tool that can help you set realistic goals and track your progress over time.

Here are some ways a 90-day plan can help you create an effective SEO strategy:

- **Set clear goals** – The first step in creating a 90-day plan is to set clear goals for what you want to achieve. These goals should be specific, measurable, and realistic. For example, you might want to increase your website traffic by 20% or improve your search engine rankings for a specific keyword.

- **Prioritize your tasks** – Once you have set your goals, it's important to prioritize the tasks that will help you achieve them. This might include things like optimizing your website's structure, creating high-quality content, or building backlinks to your site. If you have a team with you, make sure you clarify who will be working on each task.

- **Create a timeline** – With your goals and tasks in mind, you can create a timeline for the next 90 days. This will help you stay on track and ensure that you are making progress towards your SEO goals. Be sure to set deadlines for each task and build in time for review and adjustment if necessary.

- **Track your progress** – As you work through your 90-day plan, it's important to track your progress and make adjustments as needed. This will help you stay focused and ensure that you are making progress towards your goals.

- **Review and adjust** – At the end of the 90-day period, it's important to review your progress and make any necessary adjustments to your strategy. This might include revising your goals, adjusting your timeline, or tweaking your tactics.

Summary

Using a 90-day plan can be a powerful tool for creating an effective SEO strategy. By setting clear goals, prioritizing your tasks, creating a timeline, tracking your progress, and reviewing and adjusting your strategy, you can stay on track and achieve the results you are looking for.

7

Understanding Google's Algorithms

Google's SEO algorithms are a set of rules that determine how websites are ranked in search results. These algorithms are constantly updated and refined to provide users with the best possible search experience.

The main purpose of these algorithms is to ensure that the most relevant and high-quality websites are ranked at the top of search results. To do this, Google uses a variety of factors to evaluate each website and determine its relevance and authority.

Some of the factors that Google's algorithms consider include:

- **Keywords:** Google looks at the words and phrases used on a website to determine its relevance to specific search queries.

- **Content quality:** The quality of the content on a website is also important, with Google looking for high-quality, informative content that provides value to users.

- **Backlinks:** The number and quality of links pointing to a website are also taken into account, as they are seen as an indicator of the website's authority and credibility.

- **User experience:** Google also considers factors such as website speed, mobile-friendliness, and overall user experience when determining search rankings.

While the exact details of Google's algorithms are not publicly disclosed, there are some key things that you can do to optimize your site for search engines. These include:

- Conducting keyword research to identify the most relevant and valuable keywords for your website.
- Creating high-quality, informative content that provides value to users.
- Building a strong backlink profile by earning links from other high-quality websites.
- Ensuring that your website is mobile-friendly and optimized for user experience.

By following these best practices, you can improve your chances of ranking higher in search results and driving more traffic to your site.

Summary

Google's SEO algorithms play a crucial role in determining how websites are ranked in search results. By focusing on factors such as keywords, content quality, backlinks, and user experience, you can optimize your sites for search engines and improve your chances of ranking higher in search results.

8

Google's RankBrain

Google's RankBrain is an artificial intelligence (AI) algorithm that is a part of Google's search algorithm. It helps Google understand search queries and deliver more relevant search results to users.

In essence, RankBrain is a machine learning system that analyses user behaviour to help Google identify patterns and trends in search queries. This means that it can identify the intent behind a search query and provide more relevant search results based on that intent.

So, how does RankBrain impact SEO? Well, it means that we SEO professionals need to focus on creating high-quality content that satisfies the user's intent. This means that keyword stuffing and other outdated SEO tactics are no longer effective.

Instead, SEO professionals should focus on creating content that is well-written, informative, and engaging. They should also focus on optimizing their website's structure and content to ensure that it is easily readable by both users and search engines.

Another important aspect of SEO in the era of RankBrain is the use of long-tail keywords. These are longer, more specific phrases that users might use in their search queries. By targeting these keywords, SEO professionals can create content that is more closely aligned with the user's intent and more likely to rank well in search results.

Overall, RankBrain has had a significant impact on SEO. It has shifted the focus from outdated SEO tactics to a more user-focused approach that prioritizes high-quality content and a positive user experience. By keeping these factors in mind, SEO professionals can continue to improve their website's rankings and drive more traffic to their site.

9

Local VS National SEO – What's The Difference?

When it comes to SEO, there are two main approaches: local and national. When I first learned SEO, I was targeting local couples looking for a local wedding photographer. Essentially, my keyword strategy was focussed around variations of the keywords "wedding photographer kent." However, some companies serve customers on a national level. Whilst national SEO is certainly achievable, it's a lot harder and more complex; you're essentially in a battle with thousands of other businesses for the same keyword phrase, rather than a handful.

Local SEO

Local SEO is focused on optimizing your website for local search results. This involves targeting keywords and phrases that are relevant to your business and its location, such as "plumbers in London" or "pizza delivery in Manchester". The goal of local SEO is to ensure that your business appears at the top of the search engine results page (SERP) when someone searches for these types of keywords.

The benefits of local SEO are numerous. For one, it allows you to target a specific geographic area, which is especially important for small businesses that rely on local customers. By optimizing your website for local search, you can attract more local customers to your business, which can lead to more foot traffic, phone calls, and ultimately, more sales.

Another benefit of local SEO is that it is often less competitive than national SEO. This is because you are only competing with businesses in your local area, rather than the entire country. As a result, it can be easier to rank highly for local search terms, which can lead to increased visibility and traffic for your business.

National SEO

National SEO, on the other hand, is focused on optimizing your website for broader, more general search terms. This approach is often used by larger businesses that have a national or international reach, such as online retailers or travel companies.

The goal of national SEO is to rank highly for highly competitive search terms that have a high search volume, such as "cheap flights" or "best hotels".

The benefits of national SEO are also significant. For one, it allows you to reach a much larger audience than local SEO. By targeting broader search terms, you can attract customers from all over the country (or the world), which can lead to increased sales and revenue.

Another benefit of national SEO is that it can help to establish your brand as an authority in your industry. By ranking highly for competitive search terms, you can show potential customers that your business is reputable and trustworthy, which can lead to increased brand recognition and loyalty.

Which approach is right for you?

The approach that is right for you will depend on the nature of your business and its goals. If you are a small business that relies on local customers, then local SEO is likely the best approach for you. On the other hand, if you are a larger business with a national or international reach, then national SEO is likely the best approach

Of course, it is also possible to use a combination of both local and national SEO to achieve your goals. For example, you could optimize your website for both local and national search terms to attract a wider range of customers.

Summary

Both local and national SEO are important approaches to digital marketing, and each has its own unique benefits. By understanding the differences between these approaches and selecting the one that is right for your business, you can improve your search engine rankings, attract more customers, and ultimately, grow your business.

10

The Art Of Reverse Engineering

I mentioned earlier that by analysing the websites of other wedding photographers' websites who were in the top position, I was able to create a formula for successfully improving my rankings and getting to the top of Google. Reverse engineering a competitor's website that is ranking No.1 on Google is a smart move for any website owner or marketer who wants to improve their own website's ranking. Here's why it's important, how to do it, and how it can help improve your website's ranking.

Why is reverse engineering important?

- **Identify strategies that work**
  By reverse engineering your competitor's website, you can identify the strategies that are working for them. This can help you incorporate these strategies into your own website to improve your rankings.

- **Identify areas of weakness**
  By analysing your competitor's website, you can identify areas where they may be weak or where they are not fully optimizing their website. This can help you capitalize on those weaknesses and improve your own website's ranking.

- **Stay ahead of the competition**
  By monitoring your competitor's websites and staying up to date with their strategies, you can stay ahead of the competition and make necessary adjustments to your own website.

How to reverse engineer a competitor's website?

1. **Identify your competitors:** The first step is to identify your top three competitors who are ranking in the top three positions on Google for your target keywords.

2. **Analyse their website structure**: Look at their website structure, including their navigation, URL structure, and site map. This can give you an idea of how their website is organized and how they are targeting their keywords.

3. **Analyse their content**: Look at the content on their website, including their blog posts, landing pages, and product pages. Analyse how they are targeting their keywords, what type of content they are creating, and how they are presenting it to your audience.

4. **Analyse their backlink profile:** Look at their backlink

profile, including the quality and quantity of their backlinks. This can help you identify opportunities for new backlinks and how you can improve your own backlink profile.

5. **Analyse their social media presence:** Look at their social media presence, including their followers, engagement, and content. This can give you an idea of how they are engaging with their audience and how you can improve your own social media presence.

How can reverse engineering help improve your website's ranking?

By reverse engineering your competitor's website, you can identify strategies and techniques that are working for them and incorporate them into your own website. This can help improve your website's ranking by optimizing your website's structure, content, and backlink profile. It can also help you stay ahead of the competition by staying up to date with the latest SEO strategies and techniques.

Summary

Reverse engineering a competitor's website that is ranking No.1 on Google is a smart move for any website owner or marketer who wants to improve their website's ranking. By analysing your competitor's website structure, content, backlink profile, and social media presence, you can identify strategies that work, areas of weakness, and opportunities for improvement. Incorporating these strategies into your own website can help improve your website's ranking and stay ahead of the competition.

11

Using SEOQuake To Analyze The Competition

SEOQuake is a free Chrome plugin, and one of my favorite little tools that provides a wealth of information on a website's SEO performance. In this chapter, we'll explore how you can use SEOQuake to research your competition and gain insights into their SEO strategy.

What is SEOQuake?

SEOQuake is a free SEO Chrome plugin that provides a variety of metrics for any website you visit. It includes information on a website's Google PageRank, Alexa Rank, domain age, number of indexed pages, backlinks, and more.

Researching Competition with SEOQuake

One of the primary uses of SEOQuake is to research your competition. By analyzing their metrics, you can gain insights into their SEO strategy and identify areas where you can improve your own website's SEO.

Here are some ways you can use SEOQuake to research your competition:

1. **Analyze Their PageRank:** The PageRank metric measures the importance of a webpage in Google's eyes. Look at your competitors' PageRank to see how well their content is performing in search engine results pages (SERPs).

2. **Check Their Backlinks:** Use the backlinks metric to see how many links are pointing to your competitors' website. Look at the quality and relevance of these links to get an idea of where they're getting their backlinks from.

3. **Analyze Their Keyword Density:** Use the keyword density metric to see which keywords your competitors are targeting on their website. This can give you insights into their content strategy and the keywords they're prioritizing.

4. **Check Their Alexa Rank:** The Alexa Rank measures a website's traffic and popularity. Use this metric to see how well your competitors are performing compared to your own website.

Summary

SEOQuake is a powerful tool for researching your competition and gaining insights into their SEO strategy. By analyzing their metrics, you can identify areas where you can improve your own website's SEO and develop a content strategy that outperforms your competitors. Use this tool in conjunction with other SEO tools and strategies to create a comprehensive SEO plan that drives traffic and leads to your website.

12

Everything You Need To Know About Keyword Research

Before I could start optimising my wedding photography website, I had to first figure out what my potential customers would be typing into Google. For example, was it "wedding photography kent" or "wedding photographer kent" or "stylish wedding photographer kent" or "reportage wedding photography kent" etc.

Without knowing what keywords we are targeting, we cannot know how to optimise our website. It's like trying to navigate when you haven't yet selected a destination!

Keyword research essentially involves identifying the most relevant and effective keywords to target in your website's content. In this chapter, we'll cover everything you need to know about keyword research and provide some tips for conducting effective keyword research for your website.

Why is Keyword Research important?

Keyword research is important because it helps you understand what your target audience is searching for online, and the terms they're using to find information on specific topics. By identifying the keywords that are most relevant to your business or industry, you can optimize your website's content to rank higher in search engine results pages, attract more organic traffic, and increase your chances of reaching your target audience.

How to conduct Keyword Research

Define your target audience

Before you can begin your keyword research, it's essential to have a clear understanding of your target audience. Consider factors such as their age, gender, location, interests, and needs, as these can influence the terms they use when searching for information online.

Brainstorm potential keywords

Once you have a clear understanding of your target audience, brainstorm a list of potential keywords related to your business or industry. Consider using tools like Google AdWords Keyword Planner, Google Trends, and other keyword research tools to help you come up with relevant keywords and phrases.

Tip: type a keyword phrase such as "wedding photographer kent" into Google and scroll to the bottom of the page. Here you will often see a "related searches" section, which can give you some great keyword phrase examples! In this instance, Google has suggested "cheap wedding photographer kent" "best wedding photographer kent" "affordable wedding photographer kent" and "maidstone wedding photographer."

Research your competition

As mentioned in the last chapter, conducting research on your competitors can help you identify the keywords they're targeting, the type of content they're creating, and the strategies they're using to rank higher in SERPs. This information can help you refine your own keyword research and develop a more effective SEO strategy.

Evaluate keyword relevance and search volume

After identifying potential keywords, evaluate your relevance to your target audience and your search volume. Tools like Google AdWords Keyword Planner and SEMrush can help you identify the search volume and competitiveness of specific keywords, allowing you to focus on the ones that are most likely to attract your target audience. You generally want to target keyword phrases with a decent search volume, after all there's little point getting to no.1 on Google for an obscure phrase that nobody is searching for!

Refine your list of keywords

Once you've evaluated the relevance and search volume of your potential keywords, refine your list to focus on the ones that are most relevant to your target audience and have the highest search volume. Consider incorporating long-tail keywords and location-based keywords, as these can be highly effective for attracting local traffic.

Summary

Keyword research is a critical component of SEO that can help you optimize your website's content for the terms and phrases your target audience is searching for online. By conducting thorough keyword research and incorporating the most relevant and effective keywords into your content, you can improve your website's visibility, attract more organic traffic, and reach your target audience more effectively.

13

Understanding Search Intent to Get the Best Traffic

Search intent refers to the reason behind a user's search query. Understanding search intent is essential for SEO, as it helps you create content that matches the user's search query and provides them with the information they are looking for. In this chapter, we'll explore how to understand search intent and use it to get the best traffic for your website.

1. **Identify the Search Query**
   The first step in understanding search intent is to identify the search query. Look at the keywords and phrases that the user has used in their search query. This will give you an idea of what the user is looking for and the type of content they are expecting to see.

2. **Determine the Search Intent**
   Once you have identified the search query, the next step is to determine the search intent. There are four types of search intent:

- **Informational:** The user is looking for information on a particular topic.

- **Navigational:** The user is looking for a specific website or web page.

- **Transactional:** The user is looking to make a purchase or complete a transaction.

- **Commercial:** The user is looking for information on a product or service before making a purchase decision.

Understanding the search intent will help you create content that matches the user's query and provides them with the information they are looking for.

1. **Create Content That Matches Search Intent**
   Once you understand the search intent, the next step is to create content that matches it. For example, if the search intent is informational, create content that provides detailed information on the topic. If the search intent is commercial, create content that compares different products or services.

2. **Optimize for Relevant Keywords**
   Optimize your content for relevant keywords that match the search intent. This will help your content rank higher in search engine results pages (SERPs) and attract the right traffic to your website.

3. **Monitor Performance and Refine**

Finally, monitor the performance of your content and refine it as needed. Look at metrics like bounce rate, time on page, and conversions to understand how users are interacting with your content. Use this information to make adjustments to your content and improve its relevance to the user's search intent.

Summary

Understanding search intent is critical for creating content that matches the user's search query and provides them with the information they are looking for. By identifying the search query, determining the search intent, creating content that matches it, optimizing for relevant keywords, and monitoring performance, you can attract the right traffic to your website and improve your SEO.

14

What Are LSA keywords?

LSA, or Latent Semantic Analysis, is an approach to natural language processing that helps search engines understand the meaning and context behind the words used in search queries. LSA keywords are related terms that are semantically related to a particular keyword or phrase. For example, I wouldn't need a separate page on my website targeting "marriage photographer kent" – Google is smart enough to know that "marriage" and "wedding" are related keywords.

In this chapter, we will explore the importance of LSA keywords in SEO and provide some tips for incorporating them into your content.

Why are LSA keywords important in SEO?

LSA keywords are important in SEO because they help search engines better understand the context and meaning behind search queries. By incorporating LSA keywords into your content, you can signal to search engines that your content is relevant to a particular topic or subject. This can improve your chances of ranking highly in search results and drive more traffic to your website.

Tips for incorporating LSA keywords into your content

- **Expand your keyword research** - Keyword research is important for optimizing your content for LSA keywords. Use keyword research tools to find LSA keywords that are related to your primary keyword or phrase.

- **Use natural language in your content** - When writing content for your website, use natural language that is easy for readers to understand. This can help search engines better understand the meaning and context behind your content, which can improve your chances of ranking highly in search results.

- **Optimize your content for user intent** - User intent refers to the reason behind a particular search query. By optimizing your content for user intent, you can ensure that your content meets the needs of the user and is relevant to your search query. This can improve your chances of ranking highly in search results and drive more traffic to your website.

- **Use topic clusters** - Topic clusters are a grouping of related content that covers a particular topic or subject in-depth. By using topic clusters, you can signal to search engines that your website is an authoritative source of information on a particular topic or subject.

This can improve your chances of ranking highly in search results and drive more traffic to your website.

Summary

LSA keywords are an important aspect of SEO that helps search engines understand the meaning and context behind search queries. By incorporating LSA keywords into your content and following these tips for optimizing your content for LSA keywords, you can improve your chances of ranking highly in search results and drive more traffic to your website.

15

Long-tail Keyword Phrases

Long tail keywords refer to search queries that are longer and more specific than generic keywords. These phrases usually consist of three or more words, and they are highly targeted to a particular niche or topic. For example, instead of searching for "car," a long tail keyword search would be "best hybrid cars under £30,000."

Long tail keywords have become increasingly important in the world of SEO, particularly national SEO or very competitive sectors. Here are some of the benefits of using long tail keywords:

Highly Targeted Traffic
   Long tail keywords help you attract highly targeted traffic to your website. When someone searches for a specific phrase, they are more likely to be looking for exactly what you have to offer. This means that they are more likely to convert into a lead or customer.

Lower Competition

Long tail keywords are usually less competitive than generic keywords.

This means that it is easier to rank for long tail keywords on Google. Since there are fewer websites competing for these specific phrases, you have a better chance of appearing at the top of the search engine results page.

Better Conversion Rates

Because long tail keywords are more specific and targeted, they tend to attract people who are further along in the buying process. This means that they are more likely to convert into paying customers than visitors who come to your site through generic keyword searches.

When it comes to using long tail keywords in your SEO and online marketing efforts, here are some tips to keep in mind:

Do Your Research

Use keyword research tools like Google Keyword Planner, Ahrefs, or SEMrush to find relevant long tail keywords for your business. Look for phrases that have a decent amount of search volume but lower competition.

Use Long Tail Keywords in Your Content

Once you have identified your long tail keywords, use them strategically in your content. This includes your blog posts, product descriptions, and landing pages.

However, be careful not to stuff your content with too many

keywords, as this can negatively impact your SEO (we'll cover keyword stuffing in the next chapter).

Optimize Your On-Page SEO

Make sure your website is optimized for your target long tail keywords. This includes optimizing your title tags, meta descriptions, and header tags with relevant keywords.

Track Your Results

Keep track of your website's rankings and traffic to see how your long tail keyword strategy is performing. Use tools like Google Analytics or Ahrefs to monitor your website's performance.

Summary

In conclusion, long tail keywords are an important part of any SEO or online marketing strategy. By targeting these specific and highly relevant phrases, you can attract more targeted traffic, improve your conversion rates, and lower your advertising costs. Just be sure to do your research, use your keywords strategically, and track your results to ensure you are getting the best possible ROI for your efforts.

16

Keyword Stuffing

Keyword stuffing is a practice that has long been frowned upon. Simply put, keyword stuffing refers to the excessive use of keywords or phrases on a web page or in a piece of content in an attempt to manipulate search engine rankings. While this tactic may have worked in the past, search engines have evolved to become more sophisticated, and keyword stuffing is now considered a black hat SEO technique that can lead to penalties, lower rankings, and even complete de-indexing from search results (we'll go into black hat SEO in more depth later on).

Why is keyword stuffing a problem?

The idea behind keyword stuffing is simple: the more times a keyword or phrase appears on a page, the more likely it is that search engines will see that page as relevant for that particular keyword. However, search engines have become much smarter over the years and are now able to detect when webmasters are trying to manipulate their rankings with keyword stuffing. In fact, Google's algorithm is designed to penalize websites that use this technique, as it is seen as a way to artificially inflate rankings.

Keyword stuffing can also make content difficult to read and result in a poor user experience. When a web page is filled with the same keyword over and over again, it can become repetitive and confusing for users, making them more likely to leave the site in search of more readable content. This can ultimately harm a website's overall engagement metrics, such as time on site, bounce rate, and conversion rate.

What are the consequences of keyword stuffing?

The consequences of keyword stuffing can be severe. In addition to penalties from search engines, keyword stuffing can also result in a loss of credibility and trust from users. When a website's content is filled with keywords to the point of being unreadable, users are likely to view the site as spammy and untrustworthy. This can harm a brand's reputation and ultimately lead to a loss of business.

What is the best way to avoid keyword stuffing?

The best way to avoid keyword stuffing is to create high-quality content that is relevant to your target audience. Rather than focusing on keyword density, focus on creating content that is valuable, engaging, and informative.

This will not only improve the user experience but also make it more likely that your content will be shared and linked to, which can ultimately lead to higher search engine rankings.

It is also important to use keywords strategically and in a natural way. Rather than trying to cram as many keywords as possible into your content, use them in a way that makes sense and adds value. This means using synonyms, related terms, and variations of your keywords throughout your content, rather than repeating the same phrase over and over again.

Summary

Keyword stuffing is a black hat SEO technique that can harm your website's rankings, user experience, and overall reputation. By focusing on creating high-quality content that is valuable to your audience and using keywords in a strategic and natural way, you can improve your search engine rankings and build a strong online presence that is both trustworthy and authoritative.

17

SEO For E-Commerce Websites

SEO is crucial for e-commerce websites who want to improve their visibility in search engine results pages (SERPs) and drive more traffic to their online stores. Whilst SEO for an e-commerce site is a little different than service-based businesses, it is certainly possible. Here are some key SEO strategies for e-commerce websites:

- **Optimize product pages:** Product pages should include high-quality images, detailed product descriptions, and relevant keywords. It's also important to include customer reviews and ratings to establish trust and credibility.

- **Focus on site architecture:** E-commerce websites should have a logical site architecture that makes it easy for users and search engines to navigate. This includes using breadcrumbs, creating category pages, and ensuring that all pages are linked together in a logical manner.

- **Use descriptive URLs:** URLs should be descriptive and include relevant keywords to help search engines understand the content on the page.

- **Improve site speed:** Site speed is a crucial factor in both user experience and SEO. E-commerce websites should optimize images, minify CSS and JavaScript files, and use a content delivery network (CDN) to improve site speed.

- **Optimize for mobile:** With the majority of online shopping now taking place on mobile devices, it's crucial that e-commerce websites are optimized for mobile. This includes using responsive design, optimizing images for mobile, and ensuring that the checkout process is streamlined and easy to use on mobile devices.

- **Focus on local SEO:** E-commerce websites with physical locations should focus on local SEO strategies, including optimizing for Google My Business, building local citations, and using location-specific keywords.

- **Build high-quality backlinks**: Backlinks from authoritative websites can improve a website's domain authority and help to improve search rankings. E-commerce websites can build high-quality backlinks through guest blogging, influencer marketing, and other link-building strategies.

Summary

By implementing these SEO strategies, e-commerce website owners can improve their visibility in search engine results pages, drive more traffic to their online stores, and ultimately increase sales and revenue.

18

Content is King

In the world of SEO, content is king. High-quality, relevant content is one of the most important factors in improving a website's visibility in search engine results pages (SERPs). In this chapter, we'll explore the role that content plays in SEO and provide tips for creating a content strategy that can help to improve your website's search rankings.

The Role of Content in SEO

Search engines are constantly looking for the most relevant and useful content to show to their users. By creating high-quality, informative, and engaging content, you can help search engines understand the focus of your website and improve your chances of ranking higher in search results.

In addition to helping improve search rankings, high-quality content can also drive traffic to your website, establish your brand as an authority in your industry, and increase user engagement and conversion rates.

Creating a Content Strategy for SEO

A well-planned content strategy is essential for SEO success. Here are some tips for creating a content strategy that can help to improve your website's search rankings:

1. **Identify your target audience:** Before creating content, it's important to understand who your target audience is and what type of content they're looking for. This can help you to create content that is relevant and useful to your audience, which can lead to higher engagement and better search rankings.

2. **Include your keywords:** By including the keywords you identified in your earlier research within your content, you can help to improve your website's visibility in search results.

3. **Develop a content calendar:** A content calendar is a schedule that outlines the topics and types of content that you plan to create and publish over a certain period of time. This can help you to stay organized and ensure that you're consistently creating high-quality, relevant content.

4. **Use a variety of content formats:** In addition to traditional written content, you should also consider using a variety of content formats, such as videos, infographics, and podcasts. This can help to keep your audience engaged and improve your chances of ranking for different types of search queries.

5. **Optimize your content**: To ensure that your content is easily discoverable by search engines, it's important to optimize it for SEO. This includes using relevant keywords in your title tags and meta descriptions, using descriptive URLs, and using internal links to other relevant content on your website.

6. **Promote your content:** Once you've created high-quality content, it's important to promote it through social media, email marketing, and other channels. This can help to increase visibility and drive traffic to your website.

Summary

Creating high-quality, relevant content is essential for SEO success. By developing a well-planned content strategy that includes keyword research, a content calendar, a variety of content formats, and content optimization, you can improve your website's visibility in search engine results pages, drive more traffic to your website, and ultimately increase your chances of success in your industry.

19

How Long Should a Page Be for SEO?

The length of a webpage can play an important role in its SEO performance. In this chapter, we'll discuss the ideal length of a webpage for SEO and how to determine the appropriate length for your specific content.

Why Does Page Length Matter for SEO?

Search engines like Google consider many factors when determining the relevance and value of a webpage for a given search query. One of these factors is the quality and quantity of content on the page. Longer pages tend to have more opportunities to include relevant keywords and provide comprehensive information, making them more valuable to users and search engines.

However, it's important to note that page length alone is not a guaranteed indicator of quality or value. Pages with thin, repetitive, or irrelevant content can actually hurt your SEO performance.

Determining the Ideal Page Length for Your Content

There is no one-size-fits-all answer to the ideal length of a webpage for SEO. The appropriate length will vary depending on the type of content, the topic, and the needs of your audience. Here are some factors to consider when determining the ideal length for your page:

1. **User Intent:** Consider the user intent behind the search query and what type of information the user is looking for. Some queries may require more detailed, in-depth content, while others may be more straightforward.

2. **Competition:** Consider the length of the top-ranking pages for your target keyword and how your content compares. While length alone isn't the only factor that determines rankings, it can be a useful benchmark for understanding user expectations and competitive landscape.

3. **Content Quality:** Focus on providing high-quality content that fully addresses the topic at hand. Avoid fluff, repetition, or filler content, and instead provide valuable and relevant information that is useful to your target audience.

4. **Formatting and Readability:** Break up long paragraphs into shorter ones, use subheadings and bullet points to organize your content, and make sure your content is easy to read and scan.

Summary

The ideal length of a webpage for SEO will vary depending on the content and context. While longer pages tend to perform better in search engine rankings, the focus should always be on providing high-quality, relevant content that addresses user needs and interests. By considering user intent, competition, content quality, and formatting, you can determine the appropriate length for your content and improve your chances of ranking higher in search engine results pages.

20

Avoiding Duplicate Content

Duplicate content refers to content that appears on multiple web pages or websites, either intentionally or unintentionally. This can be a problem for SEO because search engines may struggle to determine which version of the content is the original or most relevant. Here's what you need to know about duplicate content, why it's bad, and how to avoid it.

Why is Duplicate Content Bad?
Duplicate content can harm your website's SEO performance in a few ways:

- Search engines may struggle to determine which version of the content is the original or most relevant, which can result in lower rankings or even penalties.

- Duplicate content can also dilute the authority of your website and make it more challenging to establish a clear and consistent brand message.

- Additionally, duplicate content can also lead to cannibalization, where multiple pages on your website compete for the same keywords, resulting in lower rankings and traffic for all pages involved.

What is Considered Duplicate Content?

Duplicate content can take many forms, including:

- Identical or near-identical content on multiple pages within a website.

- Content that is copied from other websites or sources and published on your website.

- URLs that display the same content but have different parameters or tracking codes.

- Content that is available in different formats, such as PDFs, videos, or podcasts.

How to Avoid Duplicate Content

To avoid duplicate content issues, here are some tips:

1. Create unique and original content for each page on your website and avoid copying content from other websites.

2. Use canonical tags to indicate the original source of the content, especially when dealing with similar or related

pages.

3. Avoid using boilerplate or repetitive content, such as disclaimers, privacy policies, or copyright notices, on multiple pages.

4. Use 301 redirects to redirect traffic from duplicate pages to the original or most relevant version.

5. Avoid creating multiple versions of the same content in different formats unless it adds value to the user.

Summary

Duplicate content can harm your website's SEO performance and authority, and it's essential to avoid it by creating unique and original content for each page, using canonical tags, avoiding boilerplate content, and using 301 redirects when necessary. By avoiding duplicate content, you can improve your website's SEO performance, establish a clear and consistent brand message, and provide a better user experience for your audience.

21

The Skyscraper Method for SEO Content

The Skyscraper Method is a popular approach to creating high-quality, SEO-friendly content that generates backlinks and improves your website's search engine ranking. In this chapter, we'll explore how to use the Skyscraper Method to create compelling and engaging content that drives traffic to your website.

What is the Skyscraper Method?

The Skyscraper Method was developed by Brian Dean of Backlinko. It is a content creation strategy that involves identifying popular, high-ranking content in your industry, creating content that is better and more comprehensive, and then reaching out to websites to link to your content.

Step 1: Identify Popular Content: The first step in the Skyscraper Method is to identify popular content in your industry that is ranking well on search engines. Use tools like Ahrefs, SEMrush, or Google Analytics to identify the top-performing content in your niche.

Step 2: Create Better Content: Once you have identified popular content in your niche, create content that is better and more comprehensive than the original. This means adding more depth, detail, and value to the topic. Use data, statistics, and research to back up your claims and provide more in-depth insights into the topic.

Step 3: Promote Your Content: The next step is to promote your content to your target audience. Share your content on social media, send it to your email list, and reach out to industry influencers and bloggers to let them know about your content. The goal is to get as many people as possible to read and share your content.

Step 4: Build Backlinks: The final step is to build backlinks to your content. Reach out to websites that have linked to similar content in the past and let them know about your new and improved content. Use email outreach to build relationships with other websites in your industry and ask them to link to your content.

Benefits of the Skyscraper Method

The Skyscraper Method has several benefits for SEO content creation, including:

1. **Higher search engine rankings:** By creating high-quality, comprehensive content that is better than your competitors, you increase the chances of your content ranking higher on search engines.

2. **More backlinks:** The Skyscraper Method is designed to generate backlinks to your content, which can improve your website's search engine ranking.

3. **Improved brand awareness:** By promoting your content to a wider audience, you can increase your brand's visibility and awareness.

4. **Increased website traffic:** By creating content that is valuable and engaging to your target audience, you can drive more traffic to your website.

Summary

The Skyscraper Method is a powerful content creation strategy that can help you improve your website's search engine ranking, generate backlinks, and increase your website's traffic. By identifying popular content in your industry, creating better content, promoting your content, and building backlinks, you can create high-quality, SEO-friendly content that generates real results for your business.

22

Time to E-E-A-T

E.E.A.T. stands for Experience, Expertise, Authoritativeness, and Trustworthiness, and it's a term used by Google to evaluate the quality of content and websites. Essentially, E.E.A.T. is a way for Google to determine whether a website and its content are credible and reliable sources of information.

Why is E.E.A.T. important for SEO?

Google's primary goal is to provide users with the most accurate and relevant information possible. To achieve this, it needs to ensure that the content and websites it displays in search results are of high quality, and E.E.A.T. is a way for it to do so.

Websites that demonstrate high levels of experience, expertise, authoritativeness, and trustworthiness are more likely to rank higher in search results, which can result in increased traffic and visibility.

How can you improve your E.E.A.T. score?

Here are a few tips to help improve your website's E.E.A.T. score.

Show relevant experience: Experience is a relatively new ranking factor (previously it was just E-A-T), but Google is placing increased emphasis on demonstrating real-world experience. In fact, experience is so important to Google that it's mentioned 108 times in the Quality Rating Guidelines (QRG), which is a lot!

There are a few ways to demonstrate experience on your website. One way is to include author bios that highlight the author's qualifications and experience. You can also include testimonials from other experts or customers who can vouch for the author's experience. Additionally, you can use social media to connect with other experts in your field and share your own experiences.

Here are some specific examples of how you can demonstrate experience on your website:

Author bios: Include author bios that highlight the author's qualifications and experience. For example, you could list the author's education, professional experience, and any relevant certifications.

Testimonials: Include testimonials from other experts or customers who can vouch for the author's experience. This is a great way to show that other people trust the author's expertise.

Social media: Use social media to connect with other experts in your field and share your own experiences. This is a great way to build credibility and show that you are an expert in your field.

Demonstrate expertise: Ensure that your content is written by experts in your field, and that it's accurate, informative, and provides value to your readers.

Establish authority: Build your website's authority by creating high-quality, informative content that's linked to by other credible sources.

Build trust: Demonstrate that your website and content are trustworthy by providing accurate and transparent information, and by ensuring that your website is secure and free from errors. Trust is the most critical component of E-E-A-T, Google says, "*because untrustworthy pages have low E-E-A-T no matter how Experienced, Expert, or Authoritative they may seem.*"

Improve user experience: We'll touch more on this later, but ensure that your website is easy to navigate, fast, and engaging helps to provide a positive user experience. This includes optimizing for mobile devices, ensuring that your content is accessible to all users, and minimizing distractions like pop-ups and ads.

By focusing on these factors, you can improve your website's E.E.A.T. score, which can lead to higher search rankings and increased visibility in search results.

Summary

E.E.A.T. is an important factor in SEO that can have a significant impact on your website's visibility and traffic. By focusing on creating high-quality, informative content that demonstrates experience, expertise, authority, and trustworthiness, you can improve your E.E.A.T. score and increase your chances of ranking higher in search results.

23

Understanding Google's YMYL Guidelines

Google's YMYL (Your Money or Your Life) guidelines are a set of quality guidelines that apply to certain types of websites and content. The purpose of these guidelines is to ensure that websites that deal with sensitive topics related to health, finance, or personal safety provide high-quality and accurate information to users.

Why are YMYL Guidelines Important?

YMYL guidelines are important because they help to protect users from misinformation and scams. Websites that deal with sensitive topics can have a significant impact on people's lives, and it's crucial that the information they provide is accurate and reliable.

Additionally, websites that fall under the YMYL category can be subject to additional scrutiny from Google's algorithms and human reviewers. Violating these guidelines can lead to a significant drop in search engine rankings or even removal from search results altogether.

What Falls Under the YMYL Category?
The YMYL guidelines apply to websites and content that deal with sensitive topics related to:

1. Health and medical information
2. Financial and investment information
3. Legal information
4. News and current events
5. Safety and security

Examples of YMYL websites include those that provide medical advice, financial planning services, legal information, news articles, and online shopping sites.

What are the YMYL Guidelines? Google's YMYL guidelines require that websites that fall under the YMYL category meet certain criteria to be considered high-quality and trustworthy. These guidelines include:

1. **Expertise:** Websites must be created by experts in the field or have content written by experts to ensure accuracy and reliability.

2. **Authority:** Websites must have a good reputation and be authoritative in their field. This can be demonstrated through high-quality backlinks, social proof, and other factors.

3. **Trustworthiness:** Websites must be transparent and provide clear and accurate information. This includes

disclosing any conflicts of interest or affiliations with advertisers or sponsors.

4. **User Experience:** Websites must provide a positive user experience and be easy to navigate. This includes having a clear layout, fast loading times, and no intrusive ads or pop-ups.

Summary

Google's YMYL guidelines are an important set of quality guidelines that apply to certain types of websites and content. By following these guidelines, websites can ensure that they provide accurate and reliable information to users and avoid penalties from search engine algorithms and human reviewers. If you operate a website that falls under the YMYL category, it's crucial to understand and comply with these guidelines to protect both your users and your website's search engine rankings.

24

All About Blogs

Blogging has become an essential part of SEO. I found that when I was working as a wedding photographer, by posting weekly blog articles I would drive a lot of extra traffic to my website from people finding my blog posts. Some of these would be informative, such as "how to choose a wedding photographer" or "what does a wedding photographer charge?" and others would be portfolio related, i.e. "Beautiful Kent wedding in Canterbury Cathedral."

In this chapter, we will explore the role that blogging plays in SEO, and why it is important that you have a blog on your website.

First and foremost, blogging is an excellent way to generate fresh and relevant content for your website. Search engines such as Google love fresh content, and websites that regularly update their content tend to rank higher. By regularly publishing blog posts, you are signalling to search engines that your website is active, relevant and informative, which can help improve your rankings.

Blogging also provides an opportunity to incorporate keywords naturally into your content. When writing blog posts, you can strategically use relevant keywords and phrases to target specific search queries. By doing so, you can increase the likelihood of your website appearing in relevant search results, which can drive more traffic to your website.

In addition, blogging can help you to establish yourself as an authority in your industry or niche. By providing valuable information and insights through your blog posts, you can demonstrate your expertise and build trust with your audience. This can also help to attract high-quality backlinks from other websites, which can further improve your SEO.

Furthermore, blogging can help to increase the time visitors spend on your website. When you publish high-quality blog posts, visitors are more likely to stick around to read them, which can help to reduce bounce rates and increase engagement. This, in turn, can signal to search engines that your website is providing a positive user experience, which can also help to improve your rankings.

Lastly, blogging can help to attract and retain customers. By providing valuable and informative content, you can attract potential customers to your website and keep existing customers engaged. This can help to build brand awareness and loyalty, which can ultimately lead to increased sales and revenue.

Using blog posts to answer questions and remove doubts

Before buying from you, prospective customers will nearly always conduct research online to help them make an informed decision. There are two things we absolutely **do not** want them to do:

1. Find this information from a competitor
2. Come to the conclusion that your product or service is not a good solution, and shop elsewhere.

I normally advise our clients to write a list of every question they have ever been asked, and then turn this into a blog post. For example, this could be:

"What happens if it's raining on the day of my wedding and we can't get nice photos outside?"
"What happens if my photographer falls sick on my wedding day?"
"What equipment will you use to photograph our wedding?"
"What level of editing is done to our wedding photos?"

Even though some of these questions may be awkward to answer, by doing so you are demonstrating trust and transparency to your readers and building credibility.

Summary

Blogging plays a vital role in SEO, and businesses that neglect to have a blog on their website risk falling behind competitors in search engine rankings. By regularly publishing high-quality blog posts, you can improve your rankings, attract more traffic, establish yourself as an authority, and ultimately, drive more revenue for your business.

25

Topical Relevancy

Topical relevancy is a critical aspect of SEO that has become increasingly important in recent years. Search engines are now placing greater emphasis on the relevance of content to search queries, rather than just focusing on individual keywords. In this blog post, we will explore the importance of topical relevancy in SEO and provide some tips for optimizing your website for this new trend.

What is topical relevancy?

Topical relevancy refers to the relevance of a website or webpage to a particular topic or subject. In SEO terms, it is the degree to which a website's content matches the user's search query. Search engines are now using advanced algorithms to determine the relevance of content to search queries, taking into account not only the keywords used but also the context and meaning behind those keywords. For example, if I still had my wedding photography website these, Google would know that my website was all about wedding photography and trust me as a credible source of information on this subject. However, if I started blogged about wedding catering, Google would think to itself "Eh? You're a wedding photography guy. What the hell do you know about catering?"

Why is topical relevancy important in SEO?

Topical relevancy is important in SEO because it helps search engines deliver more relevant results to users. By understanding the context and meaning behind search queries, search engines can better match users with the content they are looking for. This, in turn, leads to a better user experience, which is a top priority for search engines like Google.

Tips for optimizing your website for topical relevancy

Use semantic keywords

Semantic keywords are keywords that are related to a particular topic or subject. By using semantic keywords in your content, you can signal to search engines that your content is relevant to a particular topic or subject.

Create comprehensive content

Comprehensive content is content that covers a particular topic or subject in-depth. By creating comprehensive content, you can signal to search engines that your content is authoritative and relevant to a particular topic or subject.

Use internal linking

Internal linking is the practice of linking to other pages on your website (more on this later!) By linking to other pages on your website that are relevant to a particular topic or subject, you can signal to search engines that your website is an authoritative source of information on that topic or subject.

Build external links

External links, a.k.a backlinks (again, more on this coming later!) are links from other websites to your website. By building external links from authoritative websites that are relevant to your topic or subject, you can signal to search engines that your website is an authoritative source of information on that topic or subject.

Summary

Topical relevancy is a critical aspect of SEO that has become increasingly important in recent years. By understanding the importance of topical relevancy and following these tips for optimizing your website for this growing trend, you can improve your chances of ranking highly in search results and drive more traffic to your website.

26

What Role Do Images Play In SEO?

Images are a crucial component of any website, particularly if your product or service has a strong visual appeal! As you can imagine, as a wedding photographer my images were everything, and I obsessed over the best way to display them, as well as how to compress them as much as possible without losing quality.

Not only do images enhance the overall aesthetics of a site, but they also play a vital role in SEO. In this chapter, we will discuss the importance of images for SEO and explore strategies for optimizing images to improve website ranking and visibility.

Why Are Images Important for SEO?

Images are important for SEO because they add context to the content on a web page. They can also be used to break up text, making it more readable and engaging for visitors. Additionally, images can be optimized with alt tags and titles, which are used by search engines to understand what an image is about and how it relates to the content on the page.

Optimizing Images for SEO

To optimize images for SEO, it is important to follow a few best practices. First and foremost, choose high-quality images that are relevant to the content on the page. Use original images whenever possible, as this can help improve the overall uniqueness of your website.

Secondly, it is important to compress images to reduce file size and improve website loading speed. Large image files can slow down a website, negatively impacting the user experience and search engine ranking. There are many free tools available online that can compress images without compromising their quality, such as TinyPNG and Kraken.io.

Thirdly, use descriptive file names and alt tags that accurately describe the content of the image. This helps search engines understand the context of the image and how it relates to the content on the page. Use keywords in your alt tags, but avoid keyword stuffing as this can negatively impact your website ranking.

Finally, use a sitemap to help search engines find and index your images. A sitemap is a file that contains a list of all the pages on your website, including the images. Submitting a sitemap to Google can help improve your website's visibility and ranking.

Summary

Images are an essential component of any website and can have a significant impact on search engine optimization. By following the best practices outlined in this chapter, you can optimize your images for SEO, improve website loading speed, and enhance the user experience. With the right approach, images can be a powerful tool for improving website visibility and driving traffic to your site.

27

What Role Does Video Play In SEO?

Video has become an increasingly important aspect of digital marketing in recent years, as it has been found to be an effective tool for engaging with and retaining customers. As such, it has also become an essential part of SEO strategies. I often found I'd see an increase in enquiries after I started creating video content of my photoshoots. It not only helped showcase my work and build trust, but Google seemed to actively favour blog posts with video content embedded, particularly when the videos were uploaded and embedded from YouTube (no surprise, YouTube is owned by Google!)

Bonus tip: type "Joe Gilbert wedding photo shoot" into YouTube if you want to see an old video of 20-year-old-me in action! This video alone got nearly 70k views, resulted in numerous enquiries and bookings, and the blog post for this was my top traffic driving post for years!

In this chapter, we will explore the role that video plays in SEO, and how businesses can leverage it to improve online visibility.

First and foremost, it is important to understand that video content is highly valued by search engines like Google. In fact, videos are 50 times more likely to appear on the first page of search results than text-only pages. This means that incorporating videos into your SEO strategy can help to improve your search engine rankings, and ultimately drive more traffic to your website.

One reason for this is that video content is seen as being more valuable and engaging than other forms of content. When users watch a video, they tend to stay on the page for longer, and are more likely to share the content with others. This can lead to increased engagement with your brand, and ultimately result in more conversions.

Another factor to consider is that videos can help to diversify your content portfolio. By incorporating videos into your website, you can provide users with a more engaging and interactive experience. This can help to increase user engagement, reduce bounce rates, and ultimately improve your overall search engine rankings.

In order to optimize your videos for SEO, there are several best practices that you should follow. First and foremost, it is important to ensure that your videos are optimized for keywords that are relevant to your business. This can help to ensure that your videos are being shown to the right audience, and that they are ranking for the right search terms.

It is also important to ensure that your videos are properly structured and tagged. This includes adding relevant titles, descriptions, and tags to your videos, as well as incorporating transcripts and closed captions. These elements can help to improve the accessibility of your videos and make them more visible to search engines.

In addition to these technical optimizations, it is also important to focus on creating high-quality, engaging video content. This can help to increase user engagement and retention, which can ultimately lead to more conversions and higher search engine rankings.

Summary

Overall, video plays an important role in SEO, and can be a valuable tool for businesses looking to improve their online visibility. By incorporating videos into your SEO strategy, and optimizing them for search engines, you can increase your search engine rankings, improve user engagement, and ultimately drive more traffic and conversions to your website.

28

The Growing Voice Search Trend

Voice search wasn't a thing when I learned SEO back in 2010, but these days is a rapidly growing trend in the world of SEO, with more and more people using voice-enabled devices like smartphones and smart speakers to search for information online. As a result, businesses need to adapt their SEO strategies to ensure that they are optimized for voice search. In this chapter, we will explore the impact of voice search on SEO and provide some tips for optimizing your website for voice search.

The impact of voice search on SEO

Voice search is changing the way that people search for information online, and this has significant implications for SEO. For one, voice searches tend to be more conversational in nature, with users asking questions in a natural, human-like way. This means that you need to optimize your content to answer questions in a way that sounds natural and conversational.

Another way that voice search is impacting SEO is by changing the way that search engines display results. With voice search, users typically receive just one or two results, rather than a long list of search results. As a result, businesses need to focus on optimizing content to rank highly for featured snippets and other types of rich snippets that are more likely to be displayed in voice search results.

Tips for optimizing your website for voice search

- **Focus on natural language**
  When optimizing your content for voice search, it is important to focus on natural language. This means writing content in a way that sounds conversational and answers questions in a way that people would naturally ask them. For example, users would ask "who is the best wedding photographer in Kent?" compared to a simple text search of "wedding photographer Kent."

- **Use long-tail keywords**
  Long-tail keywords are longer, more specific search terms that are often used in voice searches. By including these types of keywords in your content, you can increase your chances of ranking highly in voice search results.

- **Optimize for featured snippets**
  Featured snippets are short, concise summaries of information that appear at the top of search results. These are the types of results that are most likely to be displayed in voice search results, so it is important to optimize your

content to rank highly for these snippets.

- **Ensure that your website is mobile-friendly**
Many voice searches are conducted on mobile devices, so it is essential that your website is mobile-friendly. This means ensuring that your website is optimized for smaller screens and that it loads quickly on mobile devices.

- **Use structured data**
Structured data is a type of code that helps search engines understand the content on your website. By using structured data to mark up your content, you can increase your chances of appearing in rich snippets and other types of search results that are more likely to be displayed in voice search results.

Summary

Voice search is changing the way that people search for information online, and businesses need to adapt their SEO strategies to ensure that they are optimized for this new trend. By focusing on natural language, using long-tail keywords, optimizing for featured snippets, ensuring that your website is mobile-friendly, and using structured data, you can improve your chances of appearing in voice search results and drive more traffic to your website.

29

An Overview of On-page SEO

On-page SEO refers to the optimization of individual web pages in order to improve your visibility and relevance in SERPs. It involves optimizing various elements on a web page, such as the content, HTML tags, and website structure, to make them more search engine friendly. In this chapter, we'll explore the basics of on-page SEO and provide some tips on how to optimize your web pages for better search engine rankings.

Implement your keywords

By including the keywords you identified earlier in your web page content, meta tags, and URL structure, you can help search engines understand the focus of your page and improve your chances of ranking higher in search results.

Optimize Page Titles and Meta Descriptions

The page title and meta description are the first things that users see in search engine results pages. Make sure your page titles and meta descriptions are relevant to your content and include your target keywords. The page title should be less than 60 characters and the meta description should be less than 155 characters.

Use Header Tags

Header tags (H1, H2, H3, etc.) are used to structure the content on a web page. They not only make the content more readable for users, but also help search engines understand the importance of each section of the page. Use the H1 tag for the main title of the page and include variations of your target keywords in H2 and H3 tags.

Optimize Image Alt Text

Search engines can't read images, so it's important to include descriptive alt text for each image on your web page. Use relevant keywords in the alt text to help search engines understand the content of the image.

Use Internal Linking

We'll go into this in more depth later, but internal linking is the process of linking to other pages on your website. This not only helps users navigate your website, but also helps search engines understand the structure and hierarchy of your website. Include internal links in your content to other relevant pages on your website.

Ensure Fast Load Times

Page speed is an important factor in both user experience and search engine rankings. Make sure your web pages load quickly by optimizing images, using a content delivery network (CDN), and minifying CSS and JavaScript files.

Ensure Mobile Responsiveness

With more and more users accessing the web on mobile devices, it's important to ensure your web pages are mobile friendly. Use a responsive design that adjusts to different screen sizes and make sure your web pages are easy to navigate on mobile devices.

Summary

On-page SEO is a critical factor in improving the visibility and relevance of your web pages in search engine results pages. By conducting keyword research, optimizing page titles and meta descriptions, using header tags, optimizing image alt text, using internal linking, ensuring fast load times, and ensuring mobile responsiveness, you can improve your chances of ranking higher in search results and driving more traffic to your website.

30

Correct Use of H1 and H2 Tags

H1 and H2 tags are important elements of a website's structure and can have a significant impact on its search engine optimization (SEO) performance. In this chapter, we'll discuss the correct use of H1 and H2 tags and their importance in SEO.

What are H1 and H2 Tags?

H1 and H2 tags are HTML tags used to indicate the headings and subheadings of a webpage. The H1 tag is typically used for the main heading of the page, while the H2 tag is used for subheadings and sections.

The correct use of H1 and H2 tags is important for two primary reasons:

1. **SEO:** Search engines use heading tags to understand the structure and content of a webpage. Proper use of H1 and H2 tags can help search engines better understand the content of your website and improve your chances of ranking higher in search engine results pages (SERPs).

2. **User Experience (UX):** H1 and H2 tags also play a role in the user experience of your website. Proper use of these tags can make your content more scannable and easier to read, improving the overall user experience of your website.

Tips for Using H1 and H2 Tags Correctly

Here are some tips for using H1 and H2 tags correctly:

1. **Use the H1 tag only once per page:** The H1 tag should be used for the main heading of the page and should appear only once per page.

2. **Use the H2 tag for subheadings:** Use the H2 tag for subheadings and section titles. Use additional H3, H4, etc. tags for further subheadings as needed.

3. **Make sure the H1 tag accurately describes the page content:** The H1 tag should accurately describe the content of the page and include your primary keyword(s) for that page.

4. **Keep H2 tags consistent:** Use H2 tags consistently throughout your page, and make sure they accurately describe the content that follows.

Summary:
Proper use of H1 and H2 tags is essential for both SEO and UX purposes. By following these tips and using these tags correctly, you can help search engines better understand your

website's content and improve the overall user experience of your website. Incorporate these best practices into your website design and content creation to improve your website's search engine rankings and attract more visitors.

31

How to Use RankMath for Wordpress SEO

Here at Red Giraffe, our favourite SEO plugin for Wordpress is RankMath; a popular WordPress SEO plugin that helps website owners optimize their content for search engines. It offers a range of features, including keyword optimization, on-page analysis, XML sitemap generation, and more. In this chapter, we will explore how to use RankMath for advanced SEO.

Installation and Configuration

The first step in using RankMath is to install and activate the plugin. Once you have installed the plugin, you will need to configure the settings to ensure that it is set up correctly.

1. **Connect to Search Console**
   The first step is to connect your website to Google Search Console. This will allow RankMath to access your website's data and provide you with valuable insights into

your SEO performance.

2. **Configure General Settings**
The next step is to configure the general settings. This includes setting up the site title and meta description, as well as configuring other settings such as social media profiles, webmaster verification, and more.

3. **Configure SEO Analysis Settings**
RankMath offers a powerful SEO analysis tool that can help you optimize your content for search engines. Configure the analysis settings to ensure that the plugin is providing you with the most accurate and relevant data.

4. **Configure Sitemap Settings**
RankMath can generate a sitemap for your website, which can help search engines crawl and index your content more effectively. Configure the sitemap settings to ensure that the sitemap is up-to-date and optimized for search engines.

5. **Configure 404 Monitoring Settings**
RankMath can also monitor your website for 404 errors, which can impact your SEO performance. Configure the 404 monitoring settings to ensure that you are notified of any broken links or pages on your website.

Keyword Optimization

One of the primary features of RankMath is keyword optimization. The plugin provides a range of tools to help you optimize your content for the keywords that matter most to your business.

1. **Keyword Suggestions**
   RankMath can suggest relevant keywords for your content based on the topic and context of your page. Use these suggestions to optimize your content for the most relevant and targeted keywords.

2. **Keyword Density Analysis**
   RankMath also offers a keyword density analysis tool that can help you ensure that your content is optimized for your target keywords. Use this tool to identify areas where you can improve your keyword density and improve your SEO performance.

3. **Focus Keyword Optimization**
   RankMath allows you to set a focus keyword for each page or post on your website. Use this feature to ensure that your content is optimized for your target keyword and that you are using it appropriately throughout the content.

On-Page Analysis

RankMath also provides a range of on-page analysis tools that can help you improve your content for search engines.

1. **Content Analysis**
   The content analysis tool can help you identify areas where you can improve your content to make it more SEO-friendly. Use this tool to identify areas where you can improve your content structure, meta tags, and more.

2. **Image Optimization**
   RankMath also offers image optimization tools to help you ensure that your images are optimized for search engines. Use this feature to optimize your images' alt tags, titles, and other important metadata.

3. **Internal Linking Suggestions**
   RankMath can also provide suggestions for internal links that can help improve your website's SEO performance. Use these suggestions to link to relevant content on your website and improve your overall SEO strategy.

Summary

RankMath is a powerful SEO plugin that can help you optimize your website for search engines. By following the steps outlined in this chapter, you can use RankMath to improve your keyword optimization, on-page analysis, and more. Remember to regularly review your SEO performance and make adjustments to your strategy as needed to ensure that your website is ranking well in search engines.

32

Landing Pages – The Secret Weapon For Keyword Variation

Landing pages are an essential component of any digital marketing campaign. They are standalone pages on your website that are designed to convert visitors into leads or customers. But did you know that landing pages can also play a crucial role in SEO? In this chapter, we'll discuss the importance of landing pages in SEO and how you can optimize your landing pages to improve your search engine rankings.

What are landing pages?

Before we dive into the relationship between landing pages and SEO, let's quickly define what a landing page is. A landing page is a standalone page on your website that is designed for a specific marketing campaign or goal. Its purpose is to encourage visitors to take a specific action, such as filling out a form or making a purchase.

Landing pages are typically created to support a specific marketing campaign or goal. They are designed to be highly focused and have a single call-to-action (CTA) to maximize conversions.

The role of landing pages in SEO

Now that we understand what landing pages are, let's talk about their role in SEO. Landing pages can play a crucial role in SEO by providing relevant, high-quality content for search engines to crawl and index.

When you create a landing page that is optimized for specific keywords or phrases, it can rank higher in search engine results pages for those keywords.

This can help to drive more targeted traffic to your website and increase your chances of converting those visitors into leads or customers.

An example of this would be on our agency website; we have separate landing pages for website design, SEO, and PPC. Each page is full of relevant content, information and related blog posts in order to be highly tailored and specific to exactly what the user is looking for.

Tips for optimizing your landing pages for SEO

Here are some tips for optimizing your landing pages for SEO:

Use targeted keywords

Use targeted keywords or phrases that are relevant to the specific campaign or goal of the landing page. Make sure to include these keywords in the page title, meta description, and throughout the content.

Provide high-quality content

Provide high-quality, relevant and focussed content that meets the needs of your target audience. This can include informative articles, how-to guides, videos, or any other type of content that provides value to your visitors.

Optimize your images

Optimize your images for search engines by using descriptive file names and alt tags that include your targeted keywords.

Use a clear, concise CTA

Make sure your landing page has a clear, concise call-to-action (CTA) that is prominently displayed on the page. This can help to increase conversions and improve the overall performance of the page.

Test and optimize

Finally, test and optimize your landing pages regularly to improve your performance. Use tools like Google Analytics to track your conversion rates and make adjustments to your landing pages as needed.

Summary

Landing pages can play a crucial role in SEO by providing relevant, high-quality content for search engines to crawl and index. By optimizing your landing pages for specific keywords or phrases, providing high-quality content, optimizing your images, using a clear, concise CTA, and testing and optimizing your pages regularly, you can improve your search engine rankings and drive more targeted traffic to your website.

33

Technical SEO

Technical SEO is the process of optimizing a website's technical infrastructure to improve its search engine rankings. Technical SEO involves identifying and fixing issues related to website structure, coding, and other technical factors that may be preventing search engines from properly crawling and indexing a website and is always one of the very first steps we take here at Red Giraffe when optimising a website for SEO. In this chapter, we will explore what technical SEO is, what it includes, and why it is essential for businesses.

What is Technical SEO?

Technical SEO refers to the technical aspects of website optimization that affect search engine rankings. Technical SEO involves optimizing website code, structure, and other technical factors to ensure that search engines can crawl and index a website easily. Technical SEO is different from other types of SEO, such as on-page SEO and off-page SEO, which focus on optimizing website content and building backlinks.

What's included in Technical SEO?

Technical SEO includes a wide range of factors that can affect a website's search engine rankings. Some of the most important technical SEO factors include:

- **Website structure:** A well-structured website with clear navigation can help search engines to understand a website's content and index it more efficiently.

- **Page speed:** A fast-loading website can improve user experience and search engine rankings.

- **Mobile responsiveness:** A mobile-responsive website that looks good on all devices can improve user experience and search engine rankings.

- **HTTPS:** A secure website with an HTTPS protocol can improve user trust and search engine rankings.

- **XML sitemap:** An XML sitemap can help search engines to crawl and index a website more efficiently. You can submit your XML directly to Google Search Console in order to tell Google which pages are on your website.

- **Robots.txt file:** A robots.txt file can tell search engines which pages to crawl and which to avoid.

Why is Technical SEO important?

Technical SEO is essential for businesses that want to improve search engine rankings and attract more organic traffic to their website. A website that is poorly optimized for technical SEO can be difficult for search engines to crawl and index, which can negatively impact search engine rankings.

Additionally, technical SEO can affect user experience, which can also impact search engine rankings. By optimizing website structure, code, and other technical factors, businesses can improve their search engine rankings, attract more organic traffic, and ultimately drive business results.

Summary

Technical SEO is an essential part of website optimization that involves optimizing website structure, code, and other technical factors to improve search engine rankings. Technical SEO is different from other types of SEO, such as on-page SEO and off-page SEO, which focus on optimizing website content and building backlinks.

By optimizing technical SEO, you can improve your search engine rankings, attract more organic traffic, and drive business results.

34

URL Structure for SEO

The URL structure of your website plays a critical role in your website's search engine ranking. A clear and concise URL structure not only helps search engines understand your website's content but also makes it easier for users to navigate your website. In this chapter, we'll explore the best practices for URL structure to improve your website's SEO.

1. **Use Descriptive URLs:** Descriptive URLs that accurately reflect the content of the page are essential for SEO. Avoid generic or irrelevant URLs that do not provide any context about the page's content. Instead, use descriptive and concise keywords in your URLs that accurately represent the content of the page.

2. **Keep URLs Simple and Consistent**: Keep your URLs simple and easy to read, and avoid using unnecessary parameters, numbers, or symbols. Also, ensure that your URL structure is consistent throughout your website. This consistency makes it easier for search engines to understand your

website's content and improves user experience.

3. **Include Target Keywords:** Including your target keywords in the URL can help improve your website's search engine ranking. However, avoid stuffing your URLs with keywords as this can be viewed as spammy by search engines and result in a penalty. Use keywords judiciously and only where they are relevant and add value to the content.

4. **Use Hyphens to Separate Words:** Use hyphens to separate words in your URLs as opposed to underscores or spaces. Hyphens make URLs more readable and help search engines understand the content of the page.

5. **Keep URLs Short:** Short URLs are easier to read and remember, and they are more likely to be clicked on by users. Aim to keep your URLs under 100 characters and avoid using long and complicated URLs that are difficult to read or remember.

6. **Use Canonical URLs:** Canonical URLs help avoid duplicate content issues and improve search engine ranking. If you have multiple URLs that lead to the same content, use a canonical tag to indicate the preferred URL to search engines.

Summary

Optimizing your URL structure for SEO can improve your website's search engine ranking and enhance user experience. By using descriptive, concise, and consistent URLs that include target keywords, use hyphens to separate words, keep URLs short, and use canonical URLs, you can create a URL structure that is easy to understand for search engines and users alike.

35

Domain Authority

When it comes to organic SEO, domain authority and competitor research are crucial elements of success. In this chapter, we'll discuss what domain authority is and introduce a free tool for researching competition.

What is Domain Authority?

Domain authority (DA) is a metric developed by Moz that measures how well a website is likely to rank in search engine results pages (SERPs). It's based on factors such as the number and quality of inbound links, the relevance of the website's content, and its overall trustworthiness. Websites with a higher DA are more likely to rank well in SERPs than those with a lower DA.

Researching Competition

Researching your competition is a critical step in developing an effective SEO strategy. By analyzing your competitors' websites, you can identify gaps in their content strategy and find opportunities to create better content.

One free tool for researching competition is Moz's Link Explorer. It allows you to enter a competitor's domain and see its DA, the number of backlinks, and the top pages on their site. You can also see the anchor text of their backlinks and the websites that are linking to them.

Another tool is Ahrefs' Site Explorer. It provides similar information, including the number of backlinks, the top pages, and the referring domains.

By using these tools, you can analyze your competitors' backlink profiles, see which keywords they're ranking for, and identify content gaps. You can then use this information to develop a content strategy that outperforms your competitors.

Summary

Domain authority and competitor research are critical elements of a successful organic SEO strategy. By understanding what domain authority is and how it's calculated, you can work to improve your own DA and boost your website's visibility in SERPs. And by using free tools like Moz's Link Explorer and Ahrefs' Site Explorer, you can research your competition and develop a content strategy that outperforms them.

36

Getting To Grips With Microschema

Microschema is a term used to describe a structured data markup that helps search engines better understand the content of a web page.

Simply put, microschema is a set of codes that you can add to your website's HTML code to provide additional information about the content on the page. This information helps search engines understand the context of the page and provides users with more accurate and relevant search results.

The use of microschema is becoming increasingly important as search engines continue to evolve and improve their algorithms to provide better search results. By providing more detailed and structured data, microschema helps search engines to better understand the content of a web page and display it in a way that is more helpful to users.

Some common types of micro schema include:

- **Article schema:** This type of schema provides information about an article, such as the headline, author, date published, and the main body of the text.

- **Product schema:** This schema is used to provide information about a product, such as its name, price, description, and reviews.

- **Local business schema:** This schema is used to provide information about a local business, such as its address, phone number, hours of operation, and reviews.

- **Recipe schema**: This schema is used to provide information about a recipe, such as the ingredients, cooking time, and nutritional information.

In order to implement microschema on a website, web developers can use a variety of tools and plugins, such as Google's Structured Data Mark-up Helper or the Yoast SEO plugin for WordPress.

Summary

Microschema is a valuable tool for web developers and SEO professionals to improve the visibility and relevance of their website in search engine results. By providing additional context and structure to web page content, microschema helps search engines to better understand and categorize web page content, ultimately leading to a better user experience for search engine users.

37

Understanding Website Engagement

In today's digital age, websites are the backbone of a business's online presence. However, merely having a website is not enough to attract and retain customers. The key is to engage with your audience effectively. Improving website engagement can benefit your business in various ways, including improving SEO results.

Here are some tips on how to improve website engagement and how it can benefit your SEO efforts:

Provide High-Quality Content
High-quality, relevant, and informative content is key to engaging with your audience. Make sure your content is well-structured and easy to read. Also, use eye-catching visuals and interactive elements to keep your audience engaged.

Improve Website Speed
Website speed is a critical factor in website engagement.

Users tend to abandon a website that takes more than a few seconds to load. Therefore, optimising your website speed helps to improve user experience and engagement.

Simplify Navigation

A website with complicated navigation can be frustrating for users. Simplify your website navigation and make it easy for users to find what they are looking for.

Encourage User Participation

Encourage user participation by adding interactive elements to your website, such as polls, surveys, quizzes, or contests. This can help to keep users engaged and encourage them to spend more time on your website.

Build Social Proof

Build social proof by showcasing customer reviews and ratings on your website. This can help to establish credibility and build trust with your audience.

Optimize for Mobile

Mobile devices account for a significant portion of website traffic. Therefore, make sure your website is optimised for mobile devices. A mobile-friendly website can help to improve engagement and keep users on your website for longer.

Improving website engagement can benefit your SEO efforts in several ways. When users spend more time on your website, it signals to search engines that your website is relevant and valuable. This can improve your search engine ranking, leading to increased organic traffic and higher visibility.

Summary

Improving website engagement is crucial for businesses looking to establish a strong online presence. By providing high-quality content, simplifying navigation, encouraging user participation, building social proof, and optimising for mobile, you can improve website engagement and boost your SEO efforts.

38

Mastering Bounce Rate for Better SEO

Bounce rate is a metric that measures the percentage of website visitors who leave a site after viewing only one page. In this chapter, we will discuss what bounce rate is, how to improve it, and why it is important for SEO.

What is Bounce Rate?

Bounce rate is a metric that measures the percentage of visitors who leave a website after only viewing one page. For example, if 100 visitors land on a website and 50 of them leave after viewing only one page, the bounce rate is 50%.

What should your bounce rate be?

A good bounce rate is subjective and depends on various factors such as the type of website, the industry, and the content. In general, a bounce rate between 26% to 40% is considered excellent, while a rate between 41% to 55% is average. However, a bounce rate above 70% is generally considered high and may indicate that there are issues with website design, content, or user experience. It is important to note that the ideal bounce rate may differ based on the goals and objectives of a website.

How to Improve Bounce Rate

Reducing bounce rate is important for improving the user experience and engagement on a website. Here are some strategies that can help reduce bounce rate:

- **Improve Website Loading Speed:** A slow-loading website can increase bounce rate. To improve website loading speed, optimize images, use a content delivery network (CDN), and minimize HTTP requests.

- **Use Clear Navigation:** Make sure your website is easy to navigate and that visitors can find what they are looking for quickly.

- **Create Engaging Content:** Engaging content can keep visitors on a website longer, reducing bounce rate. Use eye-catching headlines, subheadings, and images to make your content more engaging.

- **Optimize for Mobile:** Mobile optimization is crucial for reducing bounce rate, as more than half of all internet traffic now comes from mobile devices. Make sure your website is responsive and mobile-friendly.

Why is Bounce Rate Important for SEO?

Bounce rate is an important metric for SEO because search engines like Google use it to measure user engagement. A high bounce rate indicates that visitors are not finding what they are looking for on a website, which can negatively impact search engine rankings. On the other hand, a low bounce rate indicates that visitors are engaged with a website, which can improve search engine rankings.

Summary

Bounce rate is an important metric for measuring the user experience on a website. By following the strategies outlined in this chapter, website owners can improve the user experience, reduce bounce rate, and improve search engine rankings. Remember, reducing bounce rate is not just about SEO, it's about improving the overall user experience on a website.

39

Why Speed Matters

Website speed is a crucial factor in providing a positive user experience and improving search engine optimization. In today's fast-paced world, users expect websites to load quickly, and if a website is slow, users are likely to abandon it and go elsewhere. In this chapter, we will explore the importance of website speed in SEO.

User Experience

As mentioned in the previous chapter, website speed is a critical factor in providing a positive user experience. A slow website can be frustrating for users and can lead to a high bounce rate. Bounce rate is the percentage of users who leave a website after visiting only one page.

A high bounce rate can negatively impact a website's SEO, as search engines view it as an indicator that the website is not relevant or engaging to users. Therefore, improving website speed can help to reduce bounce rates and provide a positive user experience.

Search Engine Rankings

Website speed is also an important factor in search engine rankings. Google uses website speed as a ranking factor; websites that load quickly are more likely to rank higher. This is because search engines want to provide the best possible user experience to your users, and a fast-loading website is a key part of that experience.

Mobile Responsiveness

Website speed is especially important for mobile users. Mobile devices have smaller screens and limited processing power, so a slow website can be even more frustrating for mobile users. Additionally, mobile users are often on the go, so they expect websites to load quickly. Therefore, website speed is a crucial factor in mobile responsiveness, which is another critical ranking factor for search engines.

Crawling and Indexing

Website speed can also affect how Google crawls and indexes a website. Crawling is the process by which Google discovers new pages and content on a website, and indexing is the process by which Google stores and organizes this information. A slow website can make it more difficult for search engines to crawl and index a website, which can negatively impact its search engine rankings.

Conversions

Website speed can also affect website conversions. Conversions are the percentage of website visitors who take a desired action, such as making a purchase or filling out a form. A slow website can negatively impact conversions, as users may become frustrated and abandon the website before taking the desired action. Therefore, improving website speed can help to improve website conversions and drive business results.

How to improve your website's speed

There are several key things you can do to achieve a faster website speed. First, optimize your images by compressing them and reducing their size (*TinyPNG is a great website for this. If you're using Wordpress, the Smush or Resmush.it plugins also do a great job at reducing image size*). Second, minimize HTTP requests by combining CSS and JavaScript files and using browser caching. Third, use a content delivery network (CDN) to distribute your website's content across multiple servers worldwide, reducing the distance that data has to travel. Fourth, use a reliable and fast web hosting provider. Finally, regularly monitor your website's speed using tools like Google PageSpeed Insights, GTmetrix, and Pingdom. These tools provide insights into website speed and identify areas for improvement.

Summary

Website speed is a critical factor in providing a positive user experience, improving search engine rankings, mobile responsiveness, crawling and indexing, and conversions. Therefore, it is essential you optimize your website speed to improve your SEO and drive business results.

40

How to Speed Up Your WordPress Website

Slow loading times can lead to high bounce rates, low engagement, and lower search engine rankings. In this chapter, we'll explore how to speed up your WordPress website and improve its performance.

1. **Choose a Reliable Hosting Provider**
   The first step in speeding up your WordPress website is to choose a reliable hosting provider. Look for a provider that offers fast servers, high uptime, and good customer support. A good hosting provider can make a significant difference in your website's speed and performance.

2. **Use a Lightweight Theme**
   The theme you choose can also impact your website's speed and performance. Use a lightweight theme that is optimized for speed and performance. Avoid themes with too many features and options that you don't need.

3. **Optimize Images**

   Large images can slow down your website's loading time. Optimize images by compressing them without losing quality. Use a plugin like Smush or ShortPixel to optimize images automatically.

4. **Use a Caching Plugin**

   A caching plugin can help speed up your website by storing frequently accessed data in a cache. This means that the data doesn't have to be generated every time a user accesses the page. Use a plugin like WP Super Cache or W3 Total Cache to improve your website's speed.

5. **Minimize CSS and JavaScript**

   Minimizing CSS and JavaScript files can reduce the number of HTTP requests and improve your website's loading time. Use a plugin like WP Minify or Autoptimize to minimize CSS and JavaScript files automatically.

6. **Enable Gzip Compression**

   Gzip compression reduces the size of your website's files and makes them faster to load.

7. **Use a Content Delivery Network (CDN)**

   A CDN can improve your website's speed by distributing content across multiple servers. Use a CDN like Cloudflare or MaxCDN to improve your website's speed and performance.

Summary

Website speed is crucial for user experience and SEO. By choosing a reliable hosting provider, using a lightweight theme, optimizing images, using a caching plugin, minimizing CSS and JavaScript, enabling Gzip compression, and using a content delivery network, you can speed up your WordPress website and improve its performance.

41

Internal Linking

Internal linking is an essential aspect of SEO that often gets overlooked. Many people focus on creating quality content and building backlinks, but internal linking is equally important for optimizing your website for search engines and improving the user experience.

Internal linking refers to the practice of linking pages within your own website. By linking your pages together, you make it easier for search engines to crawl your site and understand the hierarchy and relationship between your pages. Additionally, internal linking helps users navigate your site and find relevant content.

Here are some tips for effective internal linking:

- **Create a hierarchy of pages:** Think of your website as a pyramid, with the homepage at the top and sub-pages branching out below. The pages at the top of the pyramid should be linked to the most, while the pages at the bottom should have fewer internal links.

- **Use descriptive anchor text:** Anchor text is the text that is used to create a hyperlink. Use descriptive and relevant anchor text to help search engines understand what the linked page is about.

- **Link to related content:** Link to other pages on your site that are related to the content on the current page. This will help users find more information on a specific topic and keep them on your site longer.

- **Use breadcrumb navigation:** Breadcrumb navigation is a type of internal linking that shows the user where they are on your site and allows them to easily navigate back to previous pages.

- **Link to your other pages, not just your homepage:** Many people make the mistake of only linking to their homepage. Make sure to link to other pages on your site as well.

- **Avoid linking to irrelevant content**: Internal linking should be used to provide additional information and context to the user. Avoid linking to irrelevant content, as this can confuse and frustrate users.

Summary

By following these tips, you can improve the user experience on your website and help search engines understand the structure of your site. Internal linking is an often-overlooked aspect of SEO, but it can make a big difference in how your site is ranked and how users interact with it.

42

Page Structure And Link Depth

Ok we're getting pretty technical now, but trust me, this stuff is important! Page structure and link depth are important aspects of SEO that can greatly impact the success of a website's search engine rankings, but it's another factor that's often overlooked in SEO.

In this chapter, we'll explore what page structure and link depth are, why they matter, and how to optimize them for better SEO performance.

What is page structure?
Page structure refers to the way a web page is organized and designed. This includes the use of headers, sub-headers, paragraphs, images, and other elements that make up the page's content.

Search engines use page structure to understand the content and hierarchy of a web page. By properly structuring a page with clear headings and relevant content, search engines can more easily determine what the page is about and rank it accordingly.

What is link depth?
Link depth refers to the number of clicks it takes for a user to navigate from the home page to a specific page on a website. The deeper the link depth, the further away the page is from the home page.

Search engines consider link depth when ranking a website. Pages that are buried deep within a website's structure may not be crawled as often by search engine bots and may therefore receive lower rankings.

Why do page structure and link depth matter for SEO?
A well-structured page with clear headings and relevant content is easier for search engines to understand and rank. Pages with messy or disorganized structure may confuse search engines, resulting in lower rankings.

Link depth also plays a role in SEO. Pages that are buried deep within a website's structure may receive lower rankings because search engines may not crawl them as often. This means that it's important to ensure that important pages are easily accessible from the home page.

How can you optimize page structure and link depth for SEO?
To optimize page structure for SEO, make sure that each page has a clear hierarchy of headings and subheadings. Use relevant and descriptive headings that accurately reflect the content on the page.

To optimize link depth for SEO, it's important to ensure that important pages are easily accessible from the home page within one click. This can be done by including links to key pages in the main navigation menu, creating internal links from other pages, or using breadcrumb navigation.

Additionally, it's important to regularly review and update the website's structure to ensure that it's organized and easy to navigate. This can help improve the user experience and increase the website's search engine rankings.

Summary

Page structure and link depth are important aspects of SEO that can greatly impact a website's search engine rankings. By optimizing page structure with clear headings and relevant content and ensuring that important pages are easily accessible from the home page, you can improve your SEO performance and attract more organic traffic.

43

All About Backlinks

Backlinks are an essential component of Search Engine Optimization (SEO) that can greatly impact a website's search engine ranking. In the following chapters, we'll explore what backlinks are, why they are important for SEO, and how to build a strong backlink profile.

What Are Backlinks?

Backlinks, also known as inbound links or incoming links, are links from external websites that point to your website. These links are considered "votes of confidence" that signal to Google that other websites find your content valuable and relevant. It's a bit like when you were at school – the more friends someone had, the more popular they became, and the more others wanted to be their friend? When Google sees that your website has a high number of quality backlinks, they consider your website to be authoritative and relevant, which can improve your search engine ranking.

Why Backlinks Are Important for SEO

Backlinks are one of the most important factors that search engines use to determine the relevance and authority of a website. Search engines consider backlinks as an indicator of trust and credibility. The more high-quality backlinks a website has, the more likely it is to appear at the top of the results for relevant search queries.

Backlinks also play a role in the indexing and crawling of your website. Search engine crawlers follow backlinks from one website to another, which allows them to discover new pages and content on your website. If your website has a strong backlink profile, search engines are more likely to index your pages quickly and rank them higher in search results.

Monitoring Your Backlink Profile

It's important to regularly monitor your backlink profile to ensure that you are not receiving low-quality or spammy backlinks that could harm your search engine ranking. Use a backlink monitoring tool to regularly review your backlinks and disavow any that are harmful.

Summary

Backlinks are a critical component of SEO that can greatly impact your search engine ranking. By building a strong backlink profile, you can establish your website as an authority in your industry and improve your search engine visibility. Focus on creating high-quality content, guest blogging, broken link building, participating in industry communities, and monitoring your backlink profile to build a strong and effective backlink strategy.

44

How To Build High-Quality Backlinks

When I was optimising my wedding photography website for Google all those years ago, backlinks were a fundamental part of my strategy. I'd always make sure to get a tonne of great high-quality photos of the work done by the other suppliers (flowers, cake, hair, makeup, dress etc) and I would offer these photos free of charge to the suppliers on the agreement they were happy to post these photos on their blog with a link back to my site. In this chapter, we'll explore some effective strategies for building high-quality backlinks.

Create High-Quality Content

Creating high-quality content is the best way to attract high-quality backlinks. This can include blog posts, infographics, videos, and other types of content that provide value to your audience. When you create high-quality content, other websites in your industry are more likely to link to your content as a reference.

When creating content, it's important to focus on topics that are relevant to your audience and provide unique insights. Use data and statistics to support your claims and include high-quality visuals that enhance your content.

Guest Blogging

Guest blogging involves writing content for other websites in your industry in exchange for a backlink to your website. I used to write photography-related articles that other suppliers could publish on their website, such as "the best angles to photograph your wedding dress from" or "the best lighting to show off your hair and makeup," and send these out to local suppliers. This can be a great way to build backlinks and establish yourself as an expert in your field. When selecting websites to guest blog for, choose websites that have a strong domain authority and a relevant audience.

You can check the domain authority of a website at: https://ahrefs.com/website-authority-checker

When writing guest blog posts, focus on providing valuable insights and information that will be of interest to the website's audience. Include a link to your website in the author bio or within the content if it's relevant.

Broken Link Building

Broken link building involves finding broken links on other websites and reaching out to the website owner to suggest replacing the broken link with a link to your content. This can be a time-consuming process, but it can be effective in building high-quality backlinks.

To find broken links, use a backlink analysis tool such as ahrefs (https://ahrefs.com/backlink-checker) to identify broken links on websites in your industry.

Once you have identified broken links, reach out to the website owner and suggest replacing the broken link with a link to your content. Be sure to provide a relevant link that adds value to your content.

Participate in Industry Communities

Participating in online communities, such as forums and social media groups, can help you build relationships with industry influencers. This can lead to opportunities for guest blogging and other types of backlinks.

When participating in online communities, focus on providing value to the community. Share insights and information that will be of interest to the community and be sure to include a link to your website in your profile or within your content if it's relevant.

Follow vs no-follow backlinks

Follow and no-follow backlinks are two types of backlinks that play different roles in SEO. A follow backlink is a link that passes on the "link juice" from one website to another, helping the linked website to improve its ranking. On the other hand, a no-follow backlink is a link that does not pass on the link juice and does not contribute to the linked website's ranking.

While both types of backlinks can be valuable for building a diverse link profile, follow backlinks are generally considered more valuable for SEO purposes as they can help improve a website's authority and relevance in search engine results. However, it's important to note that a mix of both follow and no-follow backlinks can provide a more natural link profile and help prevent penalties from search engines for over-optimized link building practices.

Summary

Building high-quality backlinks takes time and effort, but it's worth it for the benefits it can bring to your SEO efforts. Focus on creating high-quality content, guest blogging, broken link building, participating in industry communities, and monitoring your backlink profile to build a strong and effective backlink strategy. By building a strong backlink profile, you can establish your website as an authority in your industry and improve your search engine visibility.

45

Cleaning Your Backlink Profile

Your backlink profile is an essential aspect of your website's SEO performance, and it's crucial to regularly review and clean it up to maintain a healthy and high-quality profile. Here's what you need to know about looking at your backlink profile, how to clean up bad backlinks, and why you should do it.

How to Look at Your Backlink Profile
To look at your backlink profile, you can use a backlink analysis tool, such as Ahrefs or SEMrush. These tools provide a detailed analysis of your website's backlink profile, including the number of backlinks, referring domains, anchor text, and more. You can also use these tools to identify any bad or low-quality backlinks that may be harming your website's SEO performance.

How to Clean Up Bad Backlinks
To clean up bad backlinks, you can follow these steps:

1. **Identify low-quality or spammy backlinks:** Use a backlink analysis tool to identify any low-quality or spammy backlinks that may be harming your website's SEO performance. These backlinks may come from irrelevant or low-authority websites, link farms, or paid link schemes.

2. **Contact the website owner:** If the backlink comes from a legitimate website, you can contact the owner and request that they remove the backlink. Provide them with the details of the backlink and explain why it's harmful to your website's SEO.

3. **Disavow the backlink:** If you can't get the backlink removed, you can use the Google Disavow tool to tell Google not to consider the backlink when assessing your website's SEO performance. Use this tool with caution and only as a last resort, as it can have negative consequences if not used correctly.

Why You Should Clean Up Your Backlink Profile?
Cleaning up your backlink profile is essential for several reasons:

- **Improve your website's SEO performance:** By removing bad or low-quality backlinks, you can improve your website's SEO performance, as search engines will view your website as more authoritative and relevant.

- **Avoid penalties:** If your backlink profile contains a significant number of bad or spammy backlinks, you may be at risk of receiving a penalty from search engines, which can harm your website's rankings and traffic.

Protect your website's reputation: Your backlink profile is an essential aspect of your website's reputation, and a high-quality profile can help establish your website as a trustworthy and authoritative source in your industry.

Why you should never buy backlinks

Back when I first learned SEO in 2010, it was a case of "the more backlinks, the better!" However, once people started figuring this out, website owners started buying thousands of low-quality backlinks in bulk in order to boost their website's profile. Google soon put a stop to this with its Penguin update, launched in 2012, followed by several subsequent updates over the years.

I remember it being big news in the SEO world that a lot of high-profile websites had vanished from Google overnight! The Penguin algorithm update specifically targeted websites that engaged in manipulative link building practices, such as buying low-quality backlinks from spammy websites. The update aimed to penalize websites that used such practices, and reward those that focused on building high-quality, natural backlinks. Since the Penguin update, Google has continued to refine its algorithms to better detect and penalize websites that engage in manipulative link building practices, emphasizing the importance of ethical SEO practices for long-term success.

Buying poor quality backlinks is a risky practice that can have serious consequences for your website's SEO. Poor quality backlinks are typically links from low-quality, spammy websites that have no relevance to your website's content or industry. While these backlinks may seem like a quick and easy way to improve your website's rankings, they can actually harm your website's SEO by triggering penalties from Google. These penalties can result in your website being pushed down in search engine rankings, or even being removed from search results altogether.

Additionally, poor quality backlinks can damage your website's reputation and credibility, as they may signal to search engines and users that your website is not trustworthy or relevant to their needs. It's always best to focus on building high-quality, relevant backlinks through ethical SEO practices to ensure the long-term success of your website's SEO.

Summary

Your backlink profile is a crucial aspect of your website's SEO performance, and it's essential to regularly review and clean it up to maintain a healthy and high-quality profile. By identifying and removing bad or low-quality backlinks, you can improve your website's SEO performance, avoid penalties, and protect your website's reputation. Use a backlink analysis tool to identify any harmful backlinks and follow the steps outlined above to clean up your backlink profile effectively.

46

Building Backlinks with Wikipedia to Boost SEO

Wikipedia is one of the most authoritative websites on the internet and is often used as a reference by other websites and search engines. Building backlinks with Wikipedia can be a powerful way to improve your website's SEO. Here's how:

1. **Find Relevant Wikipedia Pages**
   The first step in building backlinks with Wikipedia is to find relevant Wikipedia pages related to your website's content. Look for pages that are related to your industry or topic and have content that is similar to what you offer on your website.

2. **Add Value to the Wikipedia Page**
   Once you've identified a relevant Wikipedia page, the next step is to add value to the page by contributing high-quality content. This could be in the form of adding additional information, correcting errors, or providing additional citations and references.

3. **Include a Relevant Backlink**
   As you contribute to the Wikipedia page, you can also include a relevant backlink to your website. This backlink should be placed in a natural and non-promotional way that adds value to the page. The anchor text of the backlink should also be relevant to the content on the page and provide context for the user and search engines.

4. **Be Transparent and Follow Wikipedia Guidelines**
   When building backlinks with Wikipedia, it's important to be transparent and follow Wikipedia's guidelines. Avoid using deceptive or manipulative tactics and be upfront about your intentions. Wikipedia is a community-driven platform, and violating their guidelines can result in your contributions being removed and may even harm your website's reputation.

5. **Monitor and Track Results**
   As with any SEO strategy, it's important to monitor and track your results. Keep track of the pages you've contributed to and the backlinks you've included. Monitor your website's traffic and search engine rankings to see if there are any improvements.

Summary

Building backlinks with Wikipedia can be a powerful way to improve your website's SEO. By contributing high-quality content and including relevant backlinks in a natural and non-promotional way, you can improve your website's authority and relevance. However, it's important to be transparent and follow Wikipedia's guidelines to avoid harming your website's reputation.

47

How To Use HARO for Link Building

HARO, or Help a Reporter Out, is a platform that connects journalists and bloggers with sources for their articles and stories. HARO can also be a powerful tool for link building and publicity for your website.

Here's how:

1. **Sign Up for HARO**
   The first step in using HARO for link building and publicity is to sign up as a source. This will allow you to receive daily emails from journalists and bloggers who are looking for sources for their articles.

2. **Respond to Relevant Queries**
   As you receive HARO emails, look for queries that are relevant to your website's content or industry. Craft a response that is informative, adds value to the article, and includes a relevant backlink to your website.

3. **Follow Up and Build Relationships**
   If a journalist or blogger uses your response in their article, follow up with a thank-you email and continue building a relationship with them. This can lead to future opportunities for link building and publicity.

4. **Monitor and Track Results**
   As with any link building or publicity strategy, it's important to monitor and track your results. Keep track of the queries you've responded to and the backlinks you've earned. Monitor your website's traffic and search engine rankings to see if there are any improvements.

5. **Stay Compliant with HARO Guidelines**
   When using HARO for link building and publicity, it's important to stay compliant with HARO's guidelines. Avoid using manipulative tactics and be upfront about your intentions. HARO is a platform that values transparency and honesty, and violating their guidelines can result in your account being suspended or even banned.

Summary

HARO can be a powerful tool for link building and publicity for your website. By responding to relevant queries, building relationships with journalists and bloggers, and monitoring your results, you can improve your website's authority and relevance. However, it's important to stay compliant with HARO's guidelines to avoid any negative consequences.

48

The Importance Of Deep Backlinks

Deep backlinking refers to the practice of building links to pages on your website other than your homepage. While many businesses and website owners focus solely on building links to their homepage, deep backlinking is becoming increasingly important in the world of SEO. In this chapter, we'll explore the benefits of deep backlinking and share some tips for implementing it on your website.

Benefits of Deep Backlinking

- **Improved user experience:** By building links to pages other than your homepage, you can help users navigate to the most relevant content on your website more easily. This can lead to a better user experience and increased engagement on your website.

- **Improved search engine visibility:** Deep backlinking can help improve the visibility of your website in Google results by increasing the authority and relevance of individual pages on your website. This can lead to higher rankings for specific keywords and phrases, which can drive more traffic to your website.

- **Diversification of link profile:** By building links to multiple pages on your website, you can create a more diverse and natural link profile. This can help prevent penalties from search engines for over-optimized link building practices and improve the overall health of your website's backlink profile.

Tips for Implementing Deep Backlinking

- **Identify target pages:** Before you start building deep backlinks, it's important to identify the pages on your website that you want to target. These may be pages that are particularly important for driving conversions or pages that have valuable content that you want to promote.

- **Create valuable content:** In order to attract backlinks to your target pages, it's important to create valuable, high-quality content that people want to link to. This may include blog posts, infographics, or other types of content that provide value to your target audience.

- **Promote your content:** Once you've created valuable content, it's important to promote it through social media, email marketing, and other channels to increase its visibility and attract backlinks.

- **Build relationships with other websites:** Building relationships with other websites in your industry can help you earn backlinks to your target pages. This may include reaching out to other websites to request backlinks, participating in industry forums and communities, and guest posting on other websites.

Summary

Deep backlinking is an important SEO strategy that can help improve the visibility and relevance of individual pages on your website. By identifying target pages, creating valuable content, promoting your content, and building relationships with other websites, you can build a diverse and natural backlink profile that improves the overall health and success of your website.

49

Understanding Tiered Backlinks

Tiered backlinks are an advanced link building strategy that involves building a network of links that point to a website or webpage in a tiered structure.

The idea behind this strategy is to create a stronger and more diverse link profile that can improve the website's SEO performance. It's a little complex to get your head around, but in a nutshell here's how tiered backlinks work:

Tier 1 Backlinks

The first tier of backlinks consists of high-quality, relevant, and authoritative links that directly point to your website. These links can come from various sources, including guest posts, resource pages, directories, social media profiles, and other relevant websites. Tier 1 backlinks should be of the highest quality and relevance to ensure that they provide the maximum benefit to the target website.

Tier 2 Backlinks

The second tier of backlinks consists of links that point to the Tier 1 backlinks. These links are typically of lower quality and relevance but can still provide value to the target website. Tier 2 backlinks can come from various sources, including forum posts, blog comments, social bookmarks, and other web 2.0 properties. These links help to boost the authority and relevance of the Tier 1 backlinks, which in turn improve the authority and ranking potential of the target website.

Tier 3 Backlinks

The third tier of backlinks consists of links that point to the Tier 2 backlinks. These links are typically of even lower quality and relevance but can still contribute to the overall link profile of the target website. Tier 3 backlinks can come from various sources, including automated link building tools, article directories, and low-quality web 2.0 properties. The goal of Tier 3 backlinks is to increase the quantity and diversity of the link profile, which can help to improve the website's SEO performance.

Summary

Tiered backlinks can be an effective link building strategy when used correctly. By building a network of high-quality, relevant, and authoritative backlinks, tiered backlinks can improve the link profile of a website, which can help to improve its SEO performance. However, it's important to avoid spammy and low-quality backlinks and to use this strategy in moderation.

50

Does linking out to other sites help SEO?

One of the questions that often comes up when discussing SEO is whether linking out to other sites helps or hurts your website's search engine rankings. Here are some things to consider when it comes to linking out:

1. **Outbound Links Can Provide Value to Your Audience**
   Linking out to other sites can provide value to your audience by giving them additional resources and information. If your website is seen as a valuable source of information, it can help improve your website's reputation and authority, which can ultimately lead to improved search engine rankings.

2. **Linking Out Can Improve Your Site's Credibility**
   Linking out to other reputable sources can help improve your website's credibility and authority. By demonstrating that you are willing to cite and link to other high-quality sources, you can establish yourself as a credible source of

information, which can help improve your search engine rankings.

3. **Linking Out Can Improve Your Site's Relevance**
Linking out to other relevant websites and resources can also help improve your site's relevance for specific keywords. By providing additional information and context around a topic, you can signal to search engines that your content is relevant and useful to users, which can improve your rankings.

4. **Linking Out Should Be Done in Moderation**
While there are benefits to linking out, it's important to do so in moderation and with discretion. Linking out too often or to low-quality or spammy sites can hurt your website's credibility and authority, which can have a negative impact on your search engine rankings.

5. **Linking Out Should Be Done with the Right Anchor Text**
When linking out to other sites, it's important to use the right anchor text. The anchor text should be relevant to the content on the page and provide context for the user and search engines. Using generic anchor text like "click here" or "read more" can dilute the relevance of the link and may not provide any value to the user or search engines.

Summary

Linking out to other sites can provide value to your audience, improve your site's credibility and relevance, and ultimately help improve your search engine rankings. However, it's important to do so in moderation, with discretion, and using the right anchor text. By doing so, you can help improve the user experience, establish your website as a credible source of information, and improve your rankings in search engines.

51

Building Citations

Citations refer to mentions of your business's name, address, and phone number (NAP) on other websites, even if they do not link back to your website. Citations are important for local businesses because they can improve your local search engine rankings and help potential customers find your business online.

Here are some tips for building high-quality citations:

Consistency is Key
Consistency is key when it comes to building citations. Ensure that your business's name, address, and phone number (NAP) are consistent across all of your online listings. This includes your website, social media profiles, and other directories.

Claim Your Google My Business Listing
Google My Business (GMB) is a free tool that allows you to manage your business's online presence on Google, including

your business's appearance on Google Maps and local search results (we'll go more into this in the next chapter). Claiming your GMB listing is essential for local businesses because it allows you to manage your business's NAP, hours of operation, and other important details.

Submit Your Business to Online Directories
Submitting your business to online directories, such as Yelp, Yellow Pages, and Bing Places, can improve your local search engine ranking and increase your online visibility. When submitting your business to online directories, ensure that your NAP information is consistent and accurate.

Monitor Your Online Reviews
Online reviews can also impact your local search engine ranking. Encourage your customers to leave reviews on your GMB listing and other online directories. Respond to both positive and negative reviews to show that you are engaged with your customers and value your feedback.

Leverage Local Citations
Local citations refer to mentions of your business's NAP on local websites, such as local news websites or chamber of commerce directories. Leverage local citations by sponsoring local events or participating in local business organizations to increase your visibility within your community.

Summary
   Citations are important for local businesses because they can improve your local search engine rankings and help potential

customers find your business online. Consistency, claiming your Google My Business listing, submitting your business to online directories, monitoring your online reviews, and leveraging local citations are all effective strategies for building high-quality citations.

By building a strong citation profile, you can establish your business as a trusted and credible source within your community.

52

Follow Vs No-follow Backlinks

In this chapter, we'll explore the differences between do follow and no follow links, and how they impact SEO.

Do Follow Links

Do follow links are links that allow search engine bots to follow the link and pass on link equity to the linked page. In other words, do follow links contribute to the linked page's search engine ranking. They are considered valuable because they signal to search engines that the linked page is trustworthy and authoritative.

No Follow Links

No follow links, on the other hand, are links that contain the rel="nofollow" attribute in the HTML code. This attribute tells search engines not to follow the link and not to pass on any link equity to the linked page. No follow links are typically used for external links that the website owner does not endorse, such as comments on blog posts or sponsored content.

How Do Follow and No Follow Links Impact SEO?

While do follow links are considered valuable for SEO, having too many do follow links can be viewed as spammy by search engines and result in a penalty. It is essential to have a balance of both do follow and no follow links to maintain a healthy link profile.

No follow links are still important for SEO, as they help diversify your link profile and can drive traffic to your website. They also help to build relationships with other websites and can lead to future opportunities for do follow links.

Summary

Both do follow and no follow links have their place in SEO. While do follow links are essential for building authority and improving search engine ranking, having too many can be viewed as spammy. No follow links are also important for diversifying your link profile and building relationships with other websites. By understanding the differences between do follow and no follow links, you can create a balanced and effective link building strategy for your website.

53

Google My Business

Google My Business (GMB), also known as the map pack, is a free tool that allows businesses to manage their online presence across Google, including search and maps. In this article, we'll explore the relevance of GMB to SEO and share tips on how to boost your GMB listing.

The Relevance of GMB to SEO

GMB is a crucial component of local SEO and plays a vital role in helping businesses appear in the map pack, the section of the search results that displays local businesses in a specific area. Having a well-optimized GMB listing can increase the visibility of your business in search results, drive traffic to your website, and improve your overall online presence.

Tips for Boosting Your GMB Listing

- **Claim and verify your listing:** The first step to boosting your GMB listing is to claim and verify your listing. This involves verifying your business information, such as your address, phone number, and website, and ensuring that it is accurate and up to date.

- **Optimize your listing:** Once you have claimed and verified your listing, it's essential to optimize it for maximum visibility. This involves optimizing your business description, selecting relevant categories, and uploading high-quality photos of your business.

- **Encourage customer reviews:** Customer reviews are a critical component of your GMB listing and can influence whether or not someone chooses to do business with you. Encourage your customers to leave reviews on your GMB listing by providing excellent customer service and following up with customers after their purchase.

- **Use GMB posts**: GMB posts are a relatively new feature that allows businesses to share updates, promotions, and events directly on their GMB listing. By using GMB posts, you can increase engagement with potential customers and improve the visibility of your listing in search results.

- **Monitor and respond to reviews:** It's essential to monitor your GMB listing for new reviews and respond to them promptly, whether they are positive or negative. Responding to reviews shows that you value your customers' feedback and can help improve your overall online reputation.

Summary

Google My Business is a critical tool for businesses looking to improve their local SEO and appear in the map pack. By claiming and verifying your listing, optimizing your listing, encouraging customer reviews, using GMB posts, and monitoring and responding to reviews, you can boost your GMB listing and improve your overall online presence.

54

What Role Does Social Media Play In SEO?

Social media has become an integral part of our lives, with billions of people worldwide using platforms such as Facebook, Twitter, Instagram, TikTok and LinkedIn. Social media has not only transformed the way we communicate with one another, but it has also changed the way businesses operate. One of the significant impacts of social media on businesses is its effect on SEO. In this chapter we will explore the role of social media in SEO.

Social Signals

Social signals refer to the likes, shares, comments, and followers a website receives on social media platforms. Search engines such as Google and Bing use social signals as a factor in their ranking algorithms. Websites that have a strong social media presence and engagement tend to rank higher in search engine results pages. Social signals indicate that a website is relevant and popular, and as a result, search engines are more likely to display it to users.

Social Media Profiles

Social media profiles are indexed by search engines, and they can appear in search results. This means that social media profiles can contribute to a business's online visibility. For instance, if a user searches for a business on Google, the search engine may display the business's Facebook or Twitter profile in the search results. Therefore, it is essential to optimize social media profiles with keywords, a business description, and a link to the website.

Backlinks

Social media can also contribute to a website's backlink profile. Backlinks are links from other websites that point to a website. Search engines view backlinks as a vote of confidence and an indicator of a website's authority. Social media platforms can generate backlinks by sharing website content or by linking to a website in a social media profile. Therefore, social media can help to build a website's backlink profile and improve its search engine ranking.

Brand Awareness

Social media can also play a role in increasing brand awareness. Social media platforms provide an opportunity for businesses to interact with customers and showcase your products and services. As a result, social media can help to build a loyal customer base and generate positive reviews and feedback. This can lead to increased brand awareness and improved search engine rankings.

Local SEO

Social media can also play a significant role in local SEO. Local businesses can use social media to promote their products and services to a local audience. Social media platforms such as Facebook and Instagram have features that allow businesses to target users based on your location. This can help local businesses to reach your target audience and improve your local search engine rankings.

Summary

Social media can play a significant role in SEO. Social signals, social media profiles, backlinks, brand awareness, and local SEO are some of the ways social media can impact SEO. Therefore, it is essential for businesses to have a strong social media presence and engagement to improve their online visibility and search engine rankings.

55

Why Reviews Are So Important

One important aspect of SEO that is often overlooked is the role of reviews. In this chapter, we'll discuss the importance of reviews in SEO and how you can use them to improve your search engine rankings.

Reviews and SEO

When it comes to SEO, reviews are a key factor in determining the relevance and authority of your website. Search engines like Google use complex algorithms to determine which websites are the most relevant and trustworthy for a particular search query.

One way they do this is by analysing the number and quality of reviews for your business.

Reviews provide search engines with valuable information about your business, such as:

- The quality of your products or services
- The level of customer service you provide
- The overall reputation of your business

All of these factors contribute to the overall trustworthiness of your website, which is a critical factor in SEO. Search engines want to provide their users with the best possible results for your search queries, and they rely heavily on user feedback to determine which websites are the most trustworthy.

How to use reviews to improve your SEO

So, how can you use reviews to improve your SEO? Here are some tips:

Encourage customers to leave reviews

The first step is to encourage your customers to leave reviews. You can do this by including a call-to-action on your website or in your email marketing campaigns. You can also incentivize customers to leave reviews by offering them discounts or other perks. We like to write to clients when we know they're happy and getting good results, usually when they first make it to the no.1 position. This is a pretty good time to ask for a review!

Monitor your reviews

It's important to monitor your reviews regularly to ensure that they are accurate and up to date. If you come across a negative review, respond to it promptly and professionally. This shows that you are committed to providing excellent customer service and can help to mitigate the impact of negative reviews on your SEO.

Use reviews to create fresh content

You can also use reviews to create fresh content for your website. For example, you could create a blog post that highlights some of your best reviews or includes customer testimonials. This can help to improve your search engine rankings by providing search engines with fresh, relevant content to crawl.

Optimize your Google My Business listing

Finally, make sure you optimize your Google My Business listing by including accurate information about your business and encouraging customers to leave reviews. This can help to improve your local SEO rankings and make it easier for customers to find your business online.

Summary

Reviews play a critical role in SEO. They provide search engines with valuable information about your business and contribute to the overall trustworthiness of your website. By encouraging customers to leave reviews, monitoring your reviews regularly, using reviews to create fresh content, and optimizing your Google My Business listing, you can improve your search engine rankings and drive more traffic to your website.

56

Tracking Your Progress

Tracking your progress in SEO is essential to understanding whether your efforts are paying off and identifying areas for improvement. Here's why tracking your progress is important and how you can do it effectively.

Why track your progress in SEO?

- **Measure the effectiveness of your strategies:** By tracking your progress, you can measure how effective your SEO strategies are and make changes as necessary.

- **Identify areas for improvement:** Tracking your progress helps you identify areas where you need to improve your SEO efforts.

- **Stay ahead of the competition:** By monitoring your progress, you can stay ahead of your competition and make necessary adjustments to your strategies.

- **Measure ROI:** By tracking your progress, you can measure the return on investment (ROI) of your SEO efforts and determine if it's worth continuing or if you need to make changes.

How to track your progress in SEO

There are a number of tools you can use to track your SEO progress, both free and paid. I'll touch on a few tools you can use to measure your progress:

Google Analytics: Google Analytics is a powerful tool that allows you to track website traffic and user behaviour. You can use it to monitor your organic search traffic, bounce rate, and other important metrics.

Google Search Console: Google Search Console provides valuable data about your website's search performance. You can use it to track your search rankings, identify crawl errors, and monitor your website's health.

Keyword Ranking Tools: Keyword ranking tools such as Ahrefs and fatjoe.com allow you to track your website's ranking for specific keywords. By monitoring your rankings, you can identify which keywords are driving traffic and which ones need improvement.

Backlink Analysis Tools: Backlink analysis tools such as ahrefs or Majestic allow you to monitor your backlink profile and identify opportunities for new backlinks. This helps improve your website's authority and ranking.

Social Media Monitoring Tools: Social media monitoring tools allow you to track mentions of your brand or website on social media. This can help you identify new opportunities for engagement and outreach.

Regular Reports: Regular reporting helps you track your progress over time and identify trends. You can use this information to make data-driven decisions and improve your SEO efforts.

Summary

Tracking your progress in SEO is essential to understanding the effectiveness of your strategies and identifying areas for improvement. By using tools like Google Analytics, Google Search Console, keyword ranking tools, backlink analysis tools, social media monitoring tools, and regular reports, you can effectively track your progress and make data-driven decisions to improve your SEO efforts.

57

Black-Hat SEO

Black-hat SEO is a set of unethical and spammy practices that violate search engine guidelines and attempts to manipulate search engine rankings. These practices can lead to short-term gains but can ultimately harm a website's long-term SEO performance. Here's what you need to know about black-hat SEO, why it's bad, what it consists of, and how to avoid it.

Why is Black-hat SEO bad?

Black-hat SEO tactics violate search engine guidelines, and they are designed to manipulate search engine rankings artificially. As a result, they can harm a website's long-term SEO performance, reputation, and even lead to penalties or getting banned from search engines.

Search engines regularly update their algorithms to detect and penalize black-hat SEO tactics, which makes these tactics less effective in the long run.

What Does Black-hat SEO Consist of?

Black-hat SEO tactics can take many forms, and they can vary in severity. Here are some common examples of black-hat SEO tactics:

- **Keyword stuffing:** Filling a webpage with irrelevant keywords to manipulate search engine rankings.

- **Cloaking:** Showing different content to search engines and users to manipulate search engine rankings.

- **Paid links:** Buying links from websites to manipulate search engine rankings.

- **Content automation:** Generating low-quality content automatically to manipulate search engine rankings.

- **Link farming:** Building low-quality backlinks from irrelevant or spammy websites to manipulate search engine rankings.

- **Hidden text:** using hidden text (e.g. white text on a white background) to cram extra keywords into your page.

How to Avoid Black-hat SEO?

To avoid black-hat SEO, it's essential to focus on ethical and sustainable SEO practices that comply with search engine guidelines. Here are some tips on how to avoid black-hat SEO:

- **Follow search engine guidelines:** Understand the guidelines and best practices provided by search engines and ensure that your website complies with them.

- **Focus on quality:** Create high-quality, relevant, and useful content that provides value to your audience.

- **Build natural links:** Focus on building high-quality and relevant backlinks through ethical link building practices such as guest posting, broken link building, and content marketing.

- **Avoid shortcuts:** Avoid shortcuts and spammy tactics that promise quick results but can harm your website's long-term SEO performance.

Summary

Black-hat SEO tactics violate search engine guidelines, and they can harm a website's long-term SEO performance, reputation, and even lead to penalties or getting banned from search engines. It's important to avoid black-hat SEO tactics and focus on ethical and sustainable SEO practices that comply with search engine guidelines. By focusing on quality content, natural link building, and avoiding shortcuts, you can achieve long-term SEO success while building a reputable online presence.

58

My Favourite Tools

SEO is a complex and ever-evolving field, but fortunately, there are many tools available to help with the process. Whether you're a beginner or a seasoned SEO professional, I've composed a list below of some of my favourite tools I use that can help you improve your website's rankings and drive more traffic to your site.

- **Google Analytics**
  Google Analytics is a free tool that provides in-depth insights into your website's traffic and user behaviour. It can help you track the effectiveness of your SEO efforts, measure key performance indicators, and identify areas for improvement.

- **SEMrush**
  SEMrush is a popular SEO tool that offers a comprehensive suite of features, including keyword research, site audits,

backlink analysis, and more. While it's a paid tool, it offers a free trial that allows you to try out its features before committing to a subscription.

- **Ahrefs**
Ahrefs is another popular SEO tool that offers a range of features, including site audits, backlink analysis, and keyword research. It's a paid tool, but it offers a 7-day trial.

- **Moz**
Moz is a well-known SEO tool that offers a range of features, including site audits, keyword research, and link analysis. It offers both free and paid versions, with the paid version offering more in-depth features and analysis.

- **Rankmath**
Rankmath is a free WordPress plugin that helps with on-page SEO optimization. It provides real-time feedback on your content's readability, meta descriptions, and keyword usage, making it easy to optimize your content for search engines.

- **Google Search Console**
Google Search Console is a free tool that provides insights into your website's performance in Google search results. It allows you to monitor your site's indexing, track your search rankings, and identify issues that may be affecting your site's visibility. It's also essential for submitting your XML sitemaps, requesting re-crawls of specific pages, and monitoring for errors.

- **Screaming Frog**
  Screaming Frog is a powerful SEO tool that crawls your website and identifies technical issues that may be affecting your SEO performance. It's a paid tool, but it offers a free version that crawls up to 500 pages.

- **Serpstat**
  Serpstat is an all-in-one SEO tool that offers a range of features, including keyword research, site audits, backlink analysis, and competitor analysis. It's a paid tool, but it offers a free version with limited features.

- **Ubersuggest**
  Ubersuggest is a free tool that offers keyword research, site audits, and backlink analysis. It provides a range of data, including keyword difficulty, search volume, and CPC (cost per click), making it easy to identify profitable keywords to target.

- **Answer The Public**
  Answer The Public is another free tool that can give you some great ideas for blog post content. You enter a keyword, and it suggests a load of questions being asked and searched for which you can use as blog post topics.

- **Surfer SEO**
  Surfer SEO is a great little paid tool that runs an analysis on the top five websites ranking for your target keyword phrase. It looks at things like word count, number of images, use of headings etc.

It's probably not cost effective to purchase all of these tools, so do your research carefully and choose the tools that will be right for your needs.

59

Using ChatGPT for SEO

ChatGPT is an AI language model that can be used to assist with various aspects of SEO, including content creation, keyword research, on-page optimization, and backlink analysis. Here are some tips for using ChatGPT to improve your SEO:

Content Creation
ChatGPT can help generate content ideas and suggest keywords to include in your content to improve its SEO value. Here's how:

- Identify the topic you want to cover in your content.
- Input the topic into ChatGPT and let it generate related ideas and questions.
- Use the generated ideas to create a more comprehensive piece of content.
- Input the keywords you want to target into ChatGPT and use the suggestions it provides to optimize your content for those keywords.

Keyword Research

ChatGPT can assist with keyword research by generating a list of related keywords and analyzing their search volume and competition level. Here's how:

- Input the main keyword you want to target into ChatGPT.
- Use the generated list of related keywords to identify other potential keywords to target.
- Input the keywords into a keyword research tool to analyze their search volume and competition level.
- Use the data to identify the best keywords to target in your content.

On-Page Optimization

ChatGPT can assist with on-page optimization by analyzing content and suggesting improvements to optimize for specific keywords. Here's how:

- Input the content you want to optimize into ChatGPT.
- Input the keywords you want to target into ChatGPT.
- Use the suggestions provided by ChatGPT to optimize your content for those keywords.
- Make sure to include the keywords in the title tag, meta description, header tags, and throughout the content.

Backlink Analysis

ChatGPT can assist with backlink analysis by analyzing the backlinks of your competitors and providing insights into their backlink strategy. Here's how:

- Input the URL of your competitor's website into ChatGPT.

- Analyze the backlinks provided by ChatGPT to identify the sources of their backlinks.
- Use the data to identify potential backlink opportunities for your own website.

Summary

ChatGPT can be a valuable tool for businesses looking to improve their SEO. By using ChatGPT for content creation, keyword research, on-page optimization, and backlink analysis, businesses can improve their website's visibility and attract more organic traffic. However, it's important to remember that ChatGPT should be used as a supplement to human expertise and not a replacement.

60

The Future Of SEO

SEO has been an essential part of digital marketing since the advent of search engines. The goal of SEO is to improve the visibility and ranking of a website in search engine results to increase organic traffic and ultimately drive business growth. With the ever-changing landscape of the internet, it is crucial to stay updated on the latest trends and developments in SEO. In this chapter, we will explore the future of SEO and how it may evolve in the coming years.

Artificial Intelligence (AI) and Machine Learning (ML)

AI and ML are revolutionizing the way search engines operate, and this trend will continue in the future. AI algorithms are becoming increasingly sophisticated and can understand user intent better than ever before. As search engines become more intelligent, it is becoming more important to create high-quality content that provides value to users. Websites that focus on delivering quality content that is tailored to the user's needs will be rewarded with higher search engine rankings.

Voice Search Optimization

Voice search is becoming more popular, and it is estimated that by 2025, nearly 75% of households will have smart speakers. Optimizing for voice search will be critical in the future, as voice search queries are usually more conversational than text-based queries. This means that websites must focus on creating content that is conversational and provides answers to questions that users may ask in a more natural language.

User Experience (UX)

User experience has always been an important factor in SEO, and it will continue to be in the future. Websites that provide an excellent user experience will be rewarded with higher search engine rankings. In the future, user experience will become even more critical as search engines will focus on ranking websites that provide a better user experience higher. Websites that are easy to navigate, load quickly, and are accessible to all users will be rewarded with higher rankings.

Mobile-First Indexing

Google has been moving towards mobile-first indexing for several years, and this trend will continue in the future. Mobile-first indexing means that Google will prioritize mobile versions of websites over desktop versions when crawling and indexing pages. Websites that are not optimized for mobile devices will be penalized in search engine rankings. In the future, it will be critical to ensure that websites are optimized for mobile devices to maintain high search engine rankings.

Content Quality and Relevance

Content quality and relevance have always been essential

factors in SEO, and this trend will continue in the future. Websites that provide high-quality content that is relevant to users' search queries will be rewarded with higher search engine rankings. In the future, it will be essential to create content that is comprehensive, engaging, and provides value to users. Websites that focus on creating quality content that satisfies users' search intent will continue to rank high in search engine results pages.

Summary

The future of SEO is bright, and there are many exciting developments that we can look forward to. As search engines become more intelligent, it is essential to focus on creating quality content that provides value to users. Websites that provide an excellent user experience, are optimized for mobile devices, and focus on voice search optimization will be rewarded with higher search engine rankings. By staying updated on the latest trends and developments in SEO, businesses can stay ahead of the curve and continue to drive growth through organic traffic.